CAKE RECIPES 2022

DELICIOUS RECIPES TO SURPRISE YOUR GUESTS

MIKE LOLLI

Table of Contents

Strawberry Mousse Gâteau 12

Yule Log 14

Easter Bonnet Cake 16

Easter Simnel Cake 17

Twelfth Night Cake 19

Microwave Apple Cake 20

Microwave Applesauce Cake 21

Microwave Apple and Walnut Cake 22

Microwave Carrot Cake 23

Microwave Carrot, Pineapple and Nut Cake 24

Microwave Spiced Bran Cakes 26

Microwave Banana and Passion Fruit Cheesecake 27

Microwave Baked Orange Cheesecake 28

Microwave Pineapple Cheesecake 29

Microwave Cherry and Nut Loaf 30

Microwave Chocolate Cake 31

Microwave Chocolate Almond Cake 32

Microwave Double Chocolate Brownies 34

Microwave Chocolate Date Bars 35

Microwave Chocolate Squares 36

Microwave Quick Coffee Cake 37

Microwave Christmas Cake 38

Microwave Crumb Cake 40

Microwave Date Bars 41

Microwave Fig Bread	42
Microwave Flapjacks	43
Microwave Fruit Cake	44
Microwave Fruit and Coconut Squares	45
Microwave Fudge Cake	46
Microwave Gingerbread	47
Microwave Ginger Bars	48
Microwave Golden Cake	49
Microwave Honey and Hazelnut Cake	50
Microwave Chewy Muesli Bars	51
Microwave Nut Cake	52
Microwave Orange Juice Cake	53
Microwave Pavlova	54
Microwave Shortcake	55
Microwave Strawberry Shortcake	56
Microwave Sponge Cake	57
Microwave Sultana Bars	58
Microwave Chocolate Biscuits	59
Microwave Coconut Cookies	60
Microwave Florentines	61
Microwave Hazelnut and Cherry Biscuits	62
Microwave Sultana Biscuits	63
Microwave Banana Bread	64
Microwave Cheese Bread	65
Microwave Walnut Loaf	66
No-bake Amaretti Cake	67
American Crispy Rice Bars	68

Apricot Squares	69
Apricot Swiss Roll Cake	70
Broken Biscuit Cakes	71
No-bake Buttermilk Cake	72
Chestnut Slice	73
Chestnut Sponge Cake	74
Chocolate and Almond Bars	76
Chocolate Crisp Cake	77
Chocolate Crumb Squares	78
Chocolate Fridge Cake	79
Chocolate and Fruit Cake	80
Chocolate and Ginger Squares	81
Luxury Chocolate and Ginger Squares	82
Honey Chocolate Cookies	83
Chocolate Layer Cake	84
Nice Chocolate Bars	85
Chocolate Praline Squares	86
Coconut Crunchies	87
Crunch Bars	88
Coconut and Raisin Crunchies	89
Coffee Milk Squares	90
No-bake Fruit Cake	91
Fruity Squares	92
Fruit and Fibre Crackles	93
Nougat Layer Cake	94
Milk and Nutmeg Squares	95
Muesli Crunch	97

Orange Mousse Squares	98
Peanut Squares	99
Peppermint Caramel Cakes	100
Rice Cookies	101
Rice and Chocolate Toffette	102
Almond Paste	103
Sugar-free Almond Paste	104
Royal Icing	105
Sugar-free Icing	106
Fondant Icing	107
Butter Icing	108
Chocolate Butter Icing	109
White Chocolate Butter Icing	110
Coffee Butter Icing	111
Lemon Butter Icing	112
Orange Butter Icing	113
Cream Cheese Icing	114
Orange Icing	115
Orange Liqueur Icing	116
Peach Cake	117
Orange and Marsala Cake	118
Peach and Pear Cake	119
Moist Pineapple Cake	120
Pineapple and Cherry Cake	121
Natal Pineapple Cake	122
Pineapple Upside-down	123
Pineapple and Walnut Cake	124

Raspberry Cake 125

Rhubarb Cake 126

Rhubarb-honey Cake... 127

Beetroot Cake 128

Carrot and Banana Cake... 129

Carrot and Apple Cake 130

Carrot and Cinnamon Cake 131

Carrot and Courgette Cake... 132

Carrot and Ginger Cake 133

Carrot and Nut Cake... 134

Carrot, Orange and Nut Cake 135

Carrot, Pineapple and Coconut Cake 136

Carrot and Pistachio Cake 137

Carrot and Walnut Cake... 138

Spiced Carrot Cake.. 139

Carrot and Brown Sugar Cake.. 141

Courgette and Marrow Cake 142

Courgette and Orange Cake 143

Spiced Courgette Cake 144

Pumpkin Cake 146

Fruited Pumpkin Cake 147

Spiced Pumpkin Roll... 148

Rhubarb and Honey Cake 150

Sweet Potato Cake.. 151

Italian Almond Cake 153

Almond and Coffee Torte 154

Almond and Honey Cake 155

Almond and Lemon Cake 156

Almond Cake with Orange 157

Rich Almond Cake 158

Swedish Macaroon Cake 159

Coconut Loaf 160

Coconut Cake 161

Golden Coconut Cake 162

Coconut Layer Cake 163

Coconut and Lemon Cake 164

Coconut New Year Cake 165

Coconut and Sultana Cake 166

Crunchy-topped Nut Cake 167

Mixed Nut Cake 168

Greek Nut Cake 169

Iced Walnut Cake 170

Walnut Cake with Chocolate Cream 171

Walnut Cake with Honey and Cinnamon 172

Almond and Honey Bars 173

Apple and Blackcurrant Crumble Bars 175

Apricot and Oatmeal Bars 176

Apricot Crunchies 177

Nutty Banana Bars 178

American Brownies 179

Chocolate Fudge Brownies 180

Walnut and Chocolate Brownies 181

Butter Bars 182

Cherry Toffee Traybake 183

Chocolate Chip Traybake	184
Cinnamon Crumble Layer	185
Gooey Cinnamon Bars	186
Coconut Bars	187
Coconut and Jam Sandwich Bars	188
Date and Apple Traybake	189
Date Slices	190
Grandma's Date Bars	191
Date and Oatmeal Bars	192
Date and Walnut Bars	193
Fig Bars	194
Flapjacks	195
Cherry Flapjacks	196
Chocolate Flapjacks	197
Fruit Flapjacks	198
Fruit and Nut Flapjacks	199
Ginger Flapjacks	200
Nutty Flapjacks	201
Sharp Lemon Shortbreads	202
Mocha and Coconut Squares	203
Hello Dolly Cookies	205
Nut and Chocolate Coconut Bars	206
Nutty Squares	207
Orange Pecan Slices	208
Parkin	209
Peanut Butter Bars	210
Picnic Slices	211

Pineapple and Coconut Bars 212

Plum Yeast Cake 213

American Pumpkin Bars 215

Quince and Almond Bars 216

Raisin Bars 218

Raspberry Oat Squares 219

Shortbread Cinnamon Meringues .... **Errore. Il segnalibro non è definito.**

Strawberry Mousse Gâteau

Makes one 23 cm/9 in cake

For the cake:

100 g/4 oz/1 cup self-raising (self-rising) flour

100 g/4 oz/½ cup butter or margarine, softened

100 g/4 oz/½ cup caster (superfine) sugar

2 eggs

For the mousse:

15 ml/1 tbsp powdered gelatine

30 ml/2 tbsp water

450 g/1 lb strawberries

3 eggs, separated

75 g/3 oz/1/3 cup caster (superfine) sugar

5 ml/1 tsp lemon juice

300 ml/½ pt/1¼ cups double (heavy) cream

30 ml/2 tbsp flaked (slivered) almonds, lightly toasted

Beat together the cake ingredients until smooth. Spoon into a greased and lined 23 cm/9 in cake tin (pan) and bake in a preheated oven at 190°C/375°F/gas mark 5 for 25 minutes until golden brown and firm to the touch. Remove from the tin and leave to cool.

To make the mousse, sprinkle the gelatine over the water in a bowl and leave until spongy. Stand the bowl in a pan of hot water and leave until dissolved. Leave to cool slightly. Meanwhile, purée 350 g/12 oz of the strawberries, then rub through a sieve (strainer) to discard the pips. Beat the egg yolks and sugar until pale and thick and the mixture trails off the whisk in ribbons. Stir in the purée, lemon juice and gelatine. Whip the cream until stiff, then fold half into the mixture. With a clean whisk and bowl, whisk the egg whites until stiff, then fold into the mixture.

Cut the sponge in half horizontally and place one half in the base of a clean cake tin (pan) lined with clingfilm (plastic wrap). Slice the remaining strawberries and arrange over the sponge, then top with the flavoured cream, and finally the second layer of cake. Press down very gently. Chill until set.

To serve, invert the gâteau on to a serving plate and remove the clingfilm (plastic wrap). Decorate with the remaining cream and garnish with the almonds.

Yule Log

Makes one

3 eggs

100 g/4 oz/½ cup caster (superfine) sugar

100 g/4 oz/1 cup plain (all-purpose) flour

50 g/2 oz/½ cup plain (semi-sweet) chocolate, grated

15 ml/1 tbsp hot water

Caster (superfine) sugar for rolling

For the icing (frosting):
175 g/6 oz/¾ cup butter or margarine, softened

350 g/12 oz/2 cups icing (confectioners') sugar, sifted

30 ml/2 tbsp warm water

30 ml/2 tbsp cocoa (unsweetened chocolate) powder To decorate:

Holly leaves and robin (optional)

Beat together the eggs and sugar in a heatproof bowl set over a pan of gently simmering water. Continue to beat until the mixture is stiff and trails off the whisk in ribbons. Remove from the heat and beat until cool. Fold in half the flour, then the chocolate, then the remaining flour, then stir in the water. Spoon into a greased and lined Swiss roll tin (jelly roll pan) and bake in a preheated oven at 220°C/425°F/gas mark 7 for about 10 minutes until firm to the touch. Sprinkle a large sheet of greaseproof (waxed) paper with caster sugar. Turn the cake out of the tin on to the paper and trim the edges. Cover with another sheet of paper and roll up loosely from the short edge.

To make the icing, cream together the butter or margarine and icing sugar, then beat in the water and cocoa. Unroll the cold cake, remove the paper and spread the cake with half the icing. Roll it up again, then ice with the remaining icing, marking it with a fork to look like a log. Sift a little icing sugar over the top and decorate as liked.

Easter Bonnet Cake

Makes one 20 cm/8 in cake

75 g/3 oz/1/3 cup muscovado sugar

3 eggs

75 g/3 oz/¾ cup self-raising (self-rising) flour

15 ml/1 tbsp cocoa (unsweetened chocolate) powder

15 ml/1 tbsp warm water

For the filling:

50 g/2 oz/¼ cup butter or margarine, softened

75 g/3 oz/½ cup icing (confectioners') sugar, sifted

For the topping:

100 g/4 oz/1 cup plain (semi-sweet) chocolate

25 g/1 oz/2 tbsp butter or margarine

Ribbon or sugar flowers (optional)

Beat together the sugar and eggs in a heatproof bowl set over a pan of gently simmering water. Continue to beat until the mixture is thick and creamy. Leave to stand for a few minutes, then remove from the heat and beat again until the mixture leaves a trail when the whisk is removed. Fold in the flour and cocoa, then stir in the water. Spoon the mixture into a greased and lined 20 cm/8 in cake tin (pan) and a greased and lined 15 cm/ 6 in cake tin. Bake in a preheated oven at 200°C/400°F/gas mark 6 for 15–20 minutes until well risen and firm to the touch. Leave to cool on a wire rack.

To make the filling, cream together the margarine and icing sugar. Use to sandwich the smaller cake on top of the larger one.

To make the topping, melt the chocolate and butter or margarine in a heatproof bowl set over a pan of gently simmering water. Spoon the topping over the cake and spread with a knife dipped in hot water so that it is completely covered. Decorate round the brim with a ribbon or sugar flowers.

Easter Simnel Cake

Makes one 20 cm/8 in cake

225 g/8 oz/1 cup butter or margarine, softened

225 g/8 oz/1 cup soft brown sugar

Grated rind of 1 lemon

4 eggs, beaten

225 g/8 oz/2 cups plain (all-purpose) flour

5 ml/1 tsp baking powder

2.5 ml/½ tsp grated nutmeg

50 g/2 oz/½ cup cornflour (cornstarch)

100 g/4 oz/2/3 cup sultanas (golden raisins)

100 g/4 oz/2/3 cup raisins

75 g/3 oz/½ cup currants

100 g/4 oz/½ cup glacé (candied) cherries, chopped

25 g/1 oz/¼ cup ground almonds

450 g/1 lb Almond Paste

30 ml/2 tbsp apricot jam (conserve)

1 egg white, beaten

Cream together the butter or mar- garine, sugar and lemon rind until pale and fluffy. Gradually beat in the eggs, then fold in the flour, baking powder, nutmeg and cornflour. Stir in the fruit and almonds. Spoon half the mixture into a greased and lined 20 cm/8 in deep cake tin (pan). Roll out half the almond paste to a circle the size of the cake and place on top of the mixture. Fill with the remaining mixture and bake in a pre-heated oven at 160°C/325°F/gas mark 3 for 2–2½ hours until golden brown. Leave to cool in the tin. When cool, turn out and wrap in greaseproof (waxed) paper. Store in an airtight container for up to three weeks if possible to mature.

To finish the cake, brush the top with the jam. Roll out three-quarters of the remaining almond paste to a 20 cm/8 in circle, neaten the edges and place on top of the cake. Roll the remaining almond paste into 11 balls (to represent the disciples without Judas). Brush the top of the cake with beaten egg white and arrange the balls around the edge of the cake, then brush them with egg white. Place under a hot grill (broiler) for a minute or so to brown it slightly.

Twelfth Night Cake

Makes one 20 cm/8 in cake

225 g/8 oz/1 cup butter or margarine, softened

225 g/8 oz/1 cup soft brown sugar

4 eggs, beaten

225 g/8 oz/2 cups plain (all-purpose) flour

5 ml/1 tsp ground mixed (apple-pie) spice

175 g/6 oz/1 cup sultanas (golden raisins)

100 g/4 oz/2/3 cup raisins

75 g/3 oz/½ cup currants

50 g/2 oz/¼ cup glacé (candied) cherries

50 g/2 oz/1/3 cup chopped mixed (candied) peel

30 ml/2 tbsp milk

12 candles to decorate

Cream together the butter or mar- garine and sugar until pale and fluffy. Gradually beat in the eggs, then fold in the flour, mixed spice, fruit and peel and mix until well blended, adding a little milk if necessary to achieve a soft mixture. Spoon into a greased and lined 20 cm/8 in cake tin (pan) and bake in a preheated oven at 180°C/350°F/gas mark 4 for 2 hours until a skewer inserted in the centre comes out clean. Leave

Microwave Apple Cake

Makes one 23 cm/9 in square

100 g/4 oz/½ cup butter or margarine, softened

100 g/4 oz/½ cup soft brown sugar

30 ml/2 tbsp golden (light corn) syrup

2 eggs, lightly beaten

225 g/8 oz/2 cups self-raising (self-rising) flour

10 ml/2 tsp ground mixed (apple-pie) spice

120 ml/4 fl oz/½ cup milk

2 cooking (tart) apples, peeled, cored and thinly sliced

15 ml/1 tbsp caster (superfine) sugar

5 ml/1 tsp ground cinnamon

Cream together the butter or margarine, brown sugar and syrup until pale and fluffy. Gradually beat in the eggs. Fold in the flour and mixed spice, then stir in the milk until you have a soft consistency. Stir in the apples. Spoon into a greased and base-lined 23 cm/9 in microwave ring mould (tube pan) and microwave on Medium for 12 minutes until firm. Allow to stand for 5 minutes, then turn out upside-down and sprinkle with the caster sugar and cinnamon.

Microwave Applesauce Cake

Makes one 20 cm/8 in cake

100 g/4 oz/½ cup butter or margarine, softened

175 g/6 oz/¾ cup soft brown sugar

1 egg, lightly beaten

175 g/6 oz/1½ cups plain (all-purpose) flour

2.5 ml/½ tsp baking powder

A pinch of salt

2.5 ml/½ tsp ground allspice

1.5 ml/¼ tsp grated nutmeg

1.5 ml/¼ tsp ground cloves

300 ml/½ pt/1¼ cups unsweetened apple purée (sauce)

75 g/3 oz/½ cup raisins

Icing (confectioner's) sugar for dusting

Cream together the butter or mar-garine and brown sugar until light and fluffy. Gradually beat in the egg, then fold in the flour, baking powder, salt and spices alternately with the apple purée and raisins. Spoon into a greased and floured 20 cm/8 in square microwave dish and microwave on High for 12 minutes. Leave to cool in the dish, then cut into squares and dust with icing sugar.

Microwave Apple and Walnut Cake

Makes one 20 cm/8 in cake

175 g/6 oz/¾ cup butter or margarine, softened

100 g/4 oz/½ cup caster (superfine) sugar

3 eggs, lightly beaten

30 ml/2 tbsp golden (light corn) syrup

Grated rind and juice of 1 lemon

175 g/6 oz/1½ cups self-raising (self-rising) flour

50 g/2 oz/½ cup walnuts, chopped

1 eating (dessert) apple, peeled, cored and chopped

100 g/4 oz/2/3 cup icing (confectioner's) sugar

30 ml/2 tbsp lemon juice

15 ml/1 tbsp water

Walnut halves to decorate

Cream together the butter or mar-garine and caster sugar until light and fluffy. Gradually add the eggs, then the syrup, lemon rind and juice. Fold in the flour, chopped nuts and apple. Spoon into a greased 20 cm/8 in round microwave dish and microwave on High for 4 minutes. Remove from the oven and cover with foil. Leave to cool. Mix the icing sugar with the lemon juice and enough of the water to form a smooth icing (frosting). Spread over the cake and decorate with walnut halves.

Microwave Carrot Cake

Makes one 18 cm/7 in cake

100 g/4 oz/½ cup butter or margarine, softened

100 g/4 oz/½ cup soft brown sugar

2 eggs, beaten

Grated rind and juice of 1 orange

2.5 ml/½ tsp ground cinnamon

A pinch of grated nutmeg

100 g/4 oz carrots, grated

100 g/4 oz/1 cup self-raising (self-rising) flour

25 g/1 oz/¼ cup ground almonds

25 g/1 oz/2 tbsp caster (superfine) sugar

For the topping:

100 g/4 oz/½ cup cream cheese

50 g/2 oz/1/3 cup icing (confectioners') sugar, sifted

30 ml/2 tbsp lemon juice

Cream together the butter and sugar until light and fluffy. Gradually beat in the eggs, then stir in the orange juice and rind, the spices and carrots. Fold in the flour, almonds and sugar. Spoon into a greased and lined 18 cm/7 in cake dish and cover with clingfilm (plastic wrap). Microwave on High for 8 minutes until a skewer inserted in the centre comes out clean. Remove the clingfilm and leave to stand for 8 minutes before turning out on to a wire rack to finish cooling. Beat the topping ingredients together, then spread over the cooled cake.

Microwave Carrot, Pineapple and Nut Cake

Makes one 20 cm/8 in cake

225 g/8 oz/1 cup caster (superfine) sugar

2 eggs

120 ml/4 fl oz/½ cup oil

1.5 ml/¼ tsp salt

5 ml/1 tsp bicarbonate of soda (baking soda)

100 g/4 oz/1 cup self-raising (self-rising) flour

5 ml/1 tsp ground cinnamon

175 g/6 oz carrots, grated

75 g/3 oz/¾ cup walnuts, chopped

225 g/8 oz crushed pineapple with its juice

For the icing (frosting):
15 g/½ oz/1 tbsp butter or margarine

50 g/2 oz/¼ cup cream cheese

10 ml/2 tsp lemon juice

Icing (confectioners') sugar, sifted

Line a large ring mould (tube pan) with baking parchment. Cream together the sugar, eggs and oil. Gently stir in the dry ingredients until well combined. Stir in the remaining cake ingredients. Pour the mixture into the prepared mould, stand it on a rack or upturned plate and microwave on High for 13 minutes or until just set. Leave to stand for 5 minutes, then turn out on to a rack to cool.

Meanwhile, make the icing. Put the butter or margarine, cream cheese and lemon juice in a bowl and microwave on High for 30–40 seconds. Gradually beat in enough icing sugar to make a thick consistency and beat until fluffy. When the cake is cold, spread over the icing.

Microwave Spiced Bran Cakes

Makes 15

75 g/3 oz/¾ cup All Bran cereal

250 ml/8 fl oz/1 cup milk

175 g/6 oz/1½ cups plain (all-purpose) flour

75 g/3 oz/1/3 cup caster (superfine) sugar

10 ml/2 tsp baking powder

10 ml/2 tsp ground mixed (apple-pie) spice

A pinch of salt

60 ml/4 tbsp golden (light corn) syrup

45 ml/3 tbsp oil

1 egg, lightly beaten

75 g/3 oz/½ cup raisins

15 ml/1 tbsp grated orange rind

Soak the cereal in the milk for 10 minutes. Mix together the flour, sugar, baking powder, mixed spice and salt, then mix into the cereal. Stir in the syrup, oil, egg, raisins and orange rind. Spoon into paper cases (cupcake papers) and microwave five cakes at a time on High for 4 minutes. Repeat for the remaining cakes.

Microwave Banana and Passion Fruit Cheesecake

Makes one 23 cm/9 in cake

100 g/4 oz/½ cup butter or margarine, melted

175 g/6 oz/1½ cups ginger biscuit (cookie) crumbs

250 g/9 oz/generous 1 cup cream cheese

175 ml/6 fl oz/¾ cup soured (dairy sour) cream

2 eggs, lightly beaten

100 g/4 oz/½ cup caster (superfine) sugar

Grated rind and juice of 1 lemon

150 ml/¼ pt/2/3 cup whipping cream

1 banana, sliced

1 passion fruit, chopped

Mix together the butter or margarine and biscuit crumbs and press into the base and sides of a 23 cm/9 in microwave flan dish. Microwave on High for 1 minute. Leave to cool.

    Beat together the cream cheese and soured cream until smooth, then beat in the egg, sugar and lemon juice and rind. Spoon into the base and spread evenly. Cook on Medium for 8 minutes. Leave to cool.

Whip the cream until stiff, then spread over the case. Top with banana slices and spoon the passion fruit flesh over the top.

Microwave Baked Orange Cheesecake

Makes one 20 cm/8 in cake

50 g/2 oz/¼ cup butter or margarine

12 digestive biscuits (Graham crackers), crushed

100 g/4 oz/½ cup caster (superfine) sugar

225 g/8 oz/1 cup cream cheese

2 eggs

30 ml/2 tbsp concentrated orange juice

15 ml/1 tbsp lemon juice

150 ml/¼ pt/2/3 cup soured (dairy sour) cream

A pinch of salt

1 orange

30 ml/2 tbsp apricot jam (conserve)

150 ml/¼ pt/2/3 cup double (heavy) cream

Melt the butter or margarine in a 20 cm/8 in microwave flan dish on High for 1 minute. Stir in the biscuit crumbs and 25 g/1 oz/2 tbsp of the sugar and press over the base and sides of the dish. Cream the cheese with the remaining sugar and the eggs, then stir in the orange and lemon juices, soured cream and salt. Spoon into the case (shell) and microwave on High for 2 minutes. Leave to stand for 2 minutes, then microwave on High for a further 2 minutes. Leave to stand for 1 minute, then microwave on High for 1 minute. Leave to cool.

Peel the orange and remove the segments from the membrane, using a sharp knife. Melt the jam and brush over the top of the cheesecake. Whip the cream and pipe round the edge of the cheesecake, then decorate with the orange segments.

Microwave Pineapple Cheesecake

Makes one 23 cm/9 in cake

100 g/4 oz/½ cup butter or margarine, melted

175 g/6 oz/1½ cups digestive biscuit (Graham cracker) crumbs

250 g/9 oz/generous 1 cup cream cheese

2 eggs, lightly beaten

5 ml/1 tsp grated lemon rind

30 ml/2 tbsp lemon juice

75 g/3 oz/1/3 cup caster (superfine) sugar

400 g/14 oz/1 large can pineapple, drained and crushed

150 ml/¼ pt/2/3 cup double (heavy) cream

Mix together the butter or margarine and biscuit crumbs and press into the base and sides of a 23 cm/9 in microwave flan dish. Microwave on High for 1 minute. Leave to cool.

> Beat together the cream cheese, eggs, lemon rind and juice and sugar until smooth. Stir in the pineapple and spoon into the base. Microwave on Medium for 6 minutes until firm. Leave to cool.

Whip the cream until stiff, then pile on top of the cheesecake.

Microwave Cherry and Nut Loaf

Makes one 900 g/2 lb loaf

175 g/6 oz/¾ cup butter or margarine, softened

175 g/6 oz/¾ cup soft brown sugar

3 eggs, beaten

225 g/8 oz/2 cups plain (all-purpose) flour

10 ml/2 tsp baking powder

A pinch of salt

45 ml/3 tbsp milk

75 g/3 oz/1/3 cup glacé (candied) cherries

75 g/3 oz/¾ cup chopped mixed nuts

25 g/1 oz/3 tbsp icing (confectioners') sugar, sifted

Cream together the butter or mar-garine and brown sugar until light and fluffy. Gradually beat in the eggs, then fold in the flour, baking powder and salt. Stir in enough of the milk to make a soft consistency, then stir in the cherries and nuts. Spoon into a greased and lined 900 g/2 lb microwave loaf dish and sprinkle with the sugar. Microwave on High for 7 minutes. Leave to stand for 5 minutes, then turn out on to a wire rack to finish cooling.

Microwave Chocolate Cake

Makes one 18 cm/7 in cake

225 g/8 oz/1 cup butter or margarine, softened

175 g/6 oz/¾ cup caster (superfine) sugar

150 g/5 oz/1¼ cups self-raising (self-rising) flour

50 g/2 oz/¼ cup cocoa (unsweetened chocolate) powder

5 ml/1 tsp baking powder

3 eggs, beaten

45 ml/3 tbsp milk

Mix together all the ingredients and spoon into a greased and lined 18 cm/7 in microwave dish. Microwave on High for 9 minutes until just firm to the touch. Leave to cool in the dish for 5 minutes, then turn out on to a wire rack to finish cooling.

Microwave Chocolate Almond Cake

Makes one 20 cm/8 in cake

For the cake:
100 g/4 oz/½ cup butter or margarine, softened

100 g/4 oz/½ cup caster (superfine) sugar

2 eggs, lightly beaten

100 g/4 oz/1 cup self-raising (self-rising) flour

50 g/2 oz/½ cup cocoa (unsweetened chocolate) powder

50 g/2 oz/½ cup ground almonds

150 ml/¼ pt/2/3 cup milk

60 ml/4 tbsp golden (light corn) syrup

For the icing (frosting):
100 g/4 oz/1 cup plain (semi-sweet) chocolate

25 g/1 oz/2 tbsp butter or margarine

8 whole almonds

To make the cake, cream together the butter or mar-garine and sugar until light and fluffy. Gradually beat in the eggs, then fold in the flour and cocoa, followed by the ground almonds. Stir in the milk and syrup and beat until light and soft. Spoon into a 20 cm/8 in microwave dish lined with clingfilm (plastic wrap) and microwave on High for 4 minutes. Remove from the oven, cover the top with foil and leave to cool slightly, then turn out on to a wire rack to finish cooling.

To make the icing, melt the chocolate and butter or margarine on High for 2 minutes. Beat well. Half-dip the almonds in the chocolate, then leave to set on a piece of greaseproof (waxed) paper. Pour the remaining icing over the cake and spread over the top and down the sides. Decorate with the almonds and leave to set.

Microwave Double Chocolate Brownies

Makes 8

150 g/5 oz/1¼ cups plain (semi-sweet) chocolate, coarsely chopped

75 g/3 oz/1/3 cup butter or margarine

175 g/6 oz/¾ cup soft brown sugar

2 eggs, lightly beaten

150 g/5 oz/1¼ cups plain (all-purpose) flour

2.5 ml/½ tsp baking powder

2.5 ml/½ tsp vanilla essence (extract)

30 ml/2 tbsp milk

Melt 50 g/2 oz/½ cup of the chocolate with the butter or margarine on High for 2 minutes. Beat in the sugar and eggs, then stir in the flour, baking powder, vanilla essence and milk until smooth. Spoon into a greased 20 cm/8 in square microwave dish and microwave on High for 7 minutes. Leave to cool in the dish for 10 minutes. Melt the remaining chocolate on High for 1 minute, then spread over the top of the cake and leave to cool. Cut into squares.

Microwave Chocolate Date Bars

Makes 8

50 g/2 oz/1/3 cup stoned (pitted) dates, chopped

60 ml/4 tbsp boiling water

65 g/2½ oz/1/3 cup butter or margarine, softened

225 g/8 oz/1 cup caster (superfine) sugar

1 egg

100 g/4 oz/1 cup plain (all-purpose) flour

10 ml/2 tsp cocoa (unsweetened chocolate) powder

2.5 ml/½ tsp baking powder

A pinch of salt

25 g/1 oz/¼ cup chopped mixed nuts

100 g/4 oz/1 cup plain (semi-sweet) chocolate, finely chopped

Mix the dates with the boiling water and leave to stand until cool. Cream together the butter or margarine with half the sugar until light and fluffy. Gradually work in the egg, then alternately fold in the flour, cocoa, baking powder and salt and the date mixture. Spoon into a greased and floured 20 cm/8 in square microwave dish. Mix the remaining sugar with the nuts and chocolate and sprinkle over the top, pressing down lightly. Microwave on High for 8 minutes. Leave to cool in the dish before cutting into squares.

Microwave Chocolate Squares

Makes 16

For the cake:

50 g/2 oz/¼ cup butter or margarine

5 ml/1 tsp caster (superfine) sugar

75 g/3 oz/¾ cup plain (all-purpose) flour

1 egg yolk

15 ml/1 tbsp water

175 g/6 oz/1½ cups plain (semi-sweet) chocolate, grated or finely chopped

For the topping:

50g /2 oz/¼ cup butter or margarine

50 g/2 oz/¼ cup caster (superfine) sugar

1 egg

2.5 ml/½ tsp vanilla essence (extract)

100 g/4 oz/1 cup walnuts, chopped

To make the cake, soften the butter or margarine and work in the sugar, flour, egg yolk and water. Spread the mixture evenly in a 20 cm/8 in square microwave dish and microwave on High for 2 minutes. Sprinkle over the chocolate and microwave on High for 1 minute. Spread evenly over the base and leave until hardened.

To make the topping, microwave the butter or margarine on High for 30 seconds. Stir in the remaining topping ingredients and spread over the chocolate. Microwave on High for 5 minutes. Leave to cool, then cut into squares.

Microwave Quick Coffee Cake

Makes one 19 cm/7 in cake

For the cake:

225 g/8 oz/1 cup butter or margarine, softened

225 g/8 oz/1 cup caster (superfine) sugar

225 g/8 oz/2 cups self-raising (self-rising) flour

5 eggs

45 ml/3 tbsp coffee essence (extract)

For the icing (frosting):

30 ml/2 tbsp coffee essence (extract)

175 g/6 oz/¾ cup butter or margarine

Icing (confectioners') sugar, sifted

Walnut halves to decorate

Mix together all the cake ingredients until well blended. Divided between two 19 cm/7 in microwave cake contain-ers and cook each one on high for 5–6 minutes. Remove from the microwave and leave to cool.

Blend together the icing ingredients, sweetening to taste with icing sugar. When cool, sandwich the cakes together with half the icing and spread the rest on top. Decorate with walnut halves.

Microwave Christmas Cake

Makes one 23 cm/9 in cake

150 g/5 oz/2/3 cup butter or margarine, softened

150 g/5 oz/2/3 cup soft brown sugar

3 eggs

30 ml/2 tbsp black treacle (molasses)

225 g/8 oz/2 cups self-raising (self-rising) flour

10 ml/2 tsp ground mixed (apple-pie) spice

2. 5 ml/½ tsp grated nutmeg

2.5 ml/½ tsp bicarbonate of soda (baking soda)

450 g/1 lb/22/3 cups mixed dried fruit (fruit cake mix)

50 g/2 oz/¼ cup glacé (candied) cherries

50 g/2 oz/1/3 cup chopped mixed peel

50 g/2 oz/½ cup chopped mixed nuts

30 ml/2 tbsp brandy

Additional brandy to mature the cake (optional)

Cream together the butter or margarine and sugar until light and fluffy. Gradually beat in the eggs and treacle, then fold in the flour, spices and bicarbonate of soda. Gently stir in the fruit, mixed peel and nuts, then stir in the brandy. Spoon into a base-lined 23 cm/9 in microwave dish and microwave on Low for 45–60 minutes. Leave to cool in the dish for 15 minutes before turning out on to a wire rack to finish cooling.

When cool, wrap the cake in foil and store in a cool, dark place for 2 weeks. If liked, pierce the top of the cake several times with a thin skewer and sprinkle over some additional brandy, then rewrap and store the cake. You can do this several times to create a richer cake.

Microwave Crumb Cake

Makes one 20 cm/8 in cake

300 g/10 oz/1¼ cups caster (superfine) sugar

225 g/8 oz/2 cups plain (all-purpose) flour

10 ml/2 tsp baking powder

5 ml/1 tsp ground cinnamon

100 g/4 oz/½ cup butter or margarine, softened

2 eggs, lightly beaten

100 ml/3½ fl oz/6½ tbsp milk

Mix together the sugar, flour, baking powder and cinnamon. Work in the butter or margarine, then set aside a quarter of the mixture. Mix together the eggs and milk and beat into the larger portion of cake mix. Spoon the mixture into a greased and floured 20 cm/8 in microwave dish and sprinkle with the reserved crumble mix. Microwave on High for 10 minutes. Leave to cool in the dish.

Microwave Date Bars

Makes 12

150 g/5 oz/1¼ cups self-raising (self-raising) flour

175 g/6 oz/¾ cup caster (superfine) sugar

100 g/4 oz/1 cup desiccated (shredded) coconut

100 g/4 oz/2/3 cups stoned (pitted) dates, chopped

50 g/2 oz/½ cup chopped mixed nuts

100 g/4 oz/½ cup butter or margarine, melted

1 egg, lightly beaten

Icing (confectioners') sugar for dusting

Mix together the dry ingredients. Stir in the butter or margarine and egg and mix to a firm dough. Press into the base of a 20 cm/8 in square microwave dish and microwave on Medium for 8 minutes until just firm. Leave in the dish for 10 minutes, then cut into bars and turn out on to a wire rack to finish cooling.

Microwave Fig Bread

Makes one 675 g/1½ lb loaf

100 g/4 oz/2 cups bran

50 g/2 oz/¼ cup soft brown sugar

45 ml/3 tbsp clear honey

100 g/4 oz/2/3 cup dried figs, chopped

50 g/2 oz/½ cup hazelnuts, chopped

300 ml/½ pt/1¼ cups milk

100 g/4 oz/1 cup wholemeal (wholewheat) flour

10 ml/2 tsp baking powder

A pinch of salt

Mix together all the ingredients to a stiff dough. Shape into a microwave loaf dish and level the surface. Cook on High for 7 minutes. Leave to cool in the dish for 10 minutes, then turn out on to a wire rack to finish cooling.

Microwave Flapjacks

Makes 24

175 g/6 oz/¾ cup butter or margarine, softened

50 g/2 oz/¼ cup caster (superfine) sugar

50 g/2 oz/¼ cup soft brown sugar

90 ml/6 tbsp golden (light corn) syrup

A pinch of salt

275 g/10 oz/2½ cups rolled oats

Mix together the butter or margarine and sugars in a large bowl and cook on High for 1 minute. Add the remaining ingredients and stir well. Spoon the mixture into a greased 18 cm/7 in microwave dish and press down lightly. Cook on High for 5 minutes. Leave to cool slightly, then cut into squares.

Microwave Fruit Cake

Makes one 18 cm/7 in cake

175 g/6 oz/¾ cup butter or margarine, softened

175 g/6 oz/¾ cup caster (superfine) sugar

Grated rind of 1 lemon

3 eggs, beaten

225 g/8 oz/2 cups plain (all-purpose) flour

5 ml/1 tsp ground mixed (apple-pie) spice

225 g/8 oz/1 1/3 cups raisins

225 g/8 oz/1 1/3 cups sultanas (golden raisins)

50 g/2 oz/¼ cup glacé (candied) cherries

50 g/2 oz/½ cup chopped mixed nuts

15 ml/1 tbsp golden (light corn) syrup

45 ml/3 tbsp brandy

Cream together the butter or mar-garine and sugar until light and fluffy. Mix in the lemon rind, then gradually beat in the eggs. Fold in the flour and mixed spice, then mix in the remaining ingredients. Spoon into a greased and lined 18 cm/7 in round microwave dish and microwave on Low for 35 minutes until a skewer inserted in the centre comes out clean. Leave to cool in the dish for 10 minutes, then turn out on to a wire rack to finish cooling.

Microwave Fruit and Coconut Squares

Makes 8

50 g/2 oz/¼ cup butter or margarine

9 digestive biscuits (Graham crackers), crushed

50 g/2 oz/½ cup desiccated (shredded) coconut

100 g/4 oz/2/3 cup chopped mixed (candied) peel

50 g/2 oz/1/3 cup stoned (pitted) dates, chopped

15 ml/1 tbsp plain (all-purpose) flour

25 g/1 oz/2 tbsp glacé (candied) cherries, chopped

100 g/4 oz/1 cup walnuts, chopped

150 ml/¼ pt/2/3 cup condensed milk

Melt the butter or margarine in a 20 cm/8 in square microwave dish on High for 40 seconds. Stir in the biscuit crumbs and spread evenly over the base of the dish. Sprinkle with the coconut, then with the mixed peel. Mix the dates with the flour, cherries and nuts and sprinkle over the top, then pour over the milk. Microwave on High for 8 minutes. Leave to cool in the dish, then cut into squares.

Microwave Fudge Cake

Makes one 20 cm/8 in cake

150 g/5 oz/1¼ cups plain (all-purpose) flour

5 ml/1 tsp baking powder

A pinch of bicarbonate of soda (baking soda)

A pinch of salt

300 g/10 oz/1¼ cups caster (superfine) sugar

50 g/2 oz/¼ cup butter or margarine, softened

250 ml/8 fl oz/1 cup milk

A few drops of vanilla essence (extract)

1 egg

100 g/4 oz /1 cup plain (semi-sweet) chocolate, chopped

50g /2 oz/½ cup chopped mixed nuts

Chocolate Butter Icing

Mix together the flour, baking powder, bicarbonate of soda and salt. Stir in the sugar, then beat in the butter or margarine, milk and vanilla essence until smooth. Beat in the egg. Microwave three-quarters of the chocolate on High for 2 minutes until melted, then beat into the cake mixture until creamy. Stir in the nuts. Spoon the mixture into two greased and floured 20 cm/8 in microwave dishes and microwave each one separately for 8 minutes. Remove from the oven, cover with foil and leave to cool for 10 minutes, then turn out on to a wire rack to finish cooling. Sandwich together with half the butter icing (frosting), then spread the remaining icing over the top and decorate with the reserved chocolate.

Microwave Gingerbread

Makes one 20 cm/8 in cake

50 g/2 oz/¼ cup butter or margarine

75 g/3 oz/¼ cup black treacle (molasses)

15 ml/1 tbsp caster (superfine) sugar

100 g/4 oz/1 cup plain (all-purpose) flour

5 ml/1 tsp ground ginger

2.5 ml/½ tsp ground mixed (apple-pie) spice

2.5 ml/½ tsp bicarbonate of soda (baking soda)

1 egg, beaten

Place the butter or margarine in a bowl and microwave on High for 30 seconds. Stir in the treacle and sugar and microwave on High for 1 minute. Stir in the flour, spices and bicarbonate of soda. Beat in the egg. Spoon the mixture into a greased 1.5 litre/2½ pint/6 cup dish and microwave on High for 4 minutes. Cool in the dish for 5 minutes, then turn out on to a wire rack to finish cooling.

Microwave Ginger Bars

Makes 12

For the cake:
150 g/5 oz/2/3 cup butter or margarine, softened

50 g/2 oz/¼ cup caster (superfine) sugar

100 g/4 oz/1 cup plain (all-purpose) flour

2.5 ml/½ tsp baking powder

5 ml/1 tsp ground ginger

For the topping:
15 g/½ oz/1 tbsp butter or margarine

15 ml/1 tbsp golden (light corn) syrup

A few drops of vanilla essence (extract)

5 ml/1 tsp ground ginger

50 g/2 oz/1/3 cup icing (confectioners') sugar

To make the cake, cream together the butter or mar-garine and sugar until light and fluffy. Stir in the flour, baking powder and ginger and mix to a smooth dough. Press into a 20 cm/8 in square microwave dish and microwave on Medium for 6 minutes until just firm.

To make the topping, melt the butter or margarine and syrup. Stir in the vanilla essence, ginger and icing sugar and whisk until thick. Spread evenly over the warm cake. Leave to cool in the dish, then cut into bars or squares.

Microwave Golden Cake

Makes one 20 cm/8 in cake

For the cake:

100 g/4 oz/½ cup butter or margarine, softened

100 g/4 oz/½ cup caster (superfine) sugar

2 eggs, lightly beaten

A few drops of vanilla essence (extract)

225 g/8 oz/2 cups plain (all-purpose) flour

10 ml/2 tsp baking powder

A pinch of salt

60 ml/4 tbsp milk

For the icing (frosting):

50 g/2 oz/¼ cup butter or margarine, softened

100 g/4 oz/2/3 cup icing (confectioner's) sugar

A few drops of vanilla essence (extract) (optional)

To make the cake, cream together the butter or margarine and sugar until light and fluffy. Gradually beat in the eggs, then fold in the flour, baking powder and salt. Stir in enough of the milk to give a soft, dropping consistency. Spoon into two greased and floured 20 cm/8 in microwave dishes and cook each cake separately on High for 6 minutes. Remove from the oven, cover with foil and leave to cool for 5 minutes, then turn out on to a wire rack to finish cooling.

To make the icing, beat the butter or margarine until soft, then beat in the icing sugar and vanilla essence, if liked. Sandwich the cakes together with half the icing, then spread the remainder over the top.

Microwave Honey and Hazelnut Cake

Makes one 18 cm/7 in cake

150 g/5 oz/2/3 cup butter or margarine, softened

100 g/4 oz/½ cup soft brown sugar

45 ml/3 tbsp clear honey

3 eggs, beaten

225 g/8 oz/2 cups self-raising (self-rising) flour

100 g/4 oz/1 cup ground hazelnuts

45 ml/3 tbsp milk

Butter Icing

Cream together the butter or margarine, sugar and honey until light and fluffy. Gradually beat in the eggs, then fold in the flour and hazelnuts and enough of the milk to give a soft consistency. Spoon into an 18 cm/7 in microwave dish and cook on Medium for 7 minutes. Leave to cool in the dish for 5 minutes, then turn out on to a wire rack to finish cooling. Cut the cake in half horizontally, then sandwich together with butter icing (frosting).

Microwave Chewy Muesli Bars

Makes about 10

100 g/4 oz/½ cup butter or margarine

175 g/6 oz/½ cup clear honey

50 g/2 oz/1/3 cup ready-to-eat dried apricots, chopped

50 g/2 oz/1/3 cup stoned (pitted) dates, chopped

75 g/3 oz/¾ cup chopped mixed nuts

100 g/4 oz/1 cup rolled oats

100 g/4 oz/½ cup soft brown sugar

1 egg, beaten

25 g/1 oz/2 tbsp self-raising (self-rising) flour

Place the butter or margarine and honey in a bowl and cook on High for 2 minutes. Mix in all the remaining ingredients. Spoon into a 20 cm/8 in microwave baking tray and microwave on High for 8 minutes. Leave to cool slightly, then cut into squares or slices.

Microwave Nut Cake

Makes one 20 cm/8 in cake

150 g/5 oz/1¼ cups plain (all-purpose) flour

A pinch of salt

5 ml/1 tsp ground cinnamon

75 g/3 oz/1/3 cup soft brown sugar

75 g/3 oz/1/3 cup caster (superfine) sugar

75 ml/5 tbsp oil

25 g/1 oz/¼ cup walnuts, chopped

5 ml/1 tsp baking powder

2.5 ml/½ tsp bicarbonate of soda (baking soda)

1 egg

150 ml/¼ pt/2/3 cup soured milk

Mix together the flour, salt and half the cinnamon. Stir in the sugars, then beat in the oil until well mixed. Remove 90 ml/6 tbsp of the mixture and stir it into the nuts and remaining cinnamon. Add the baking powder, bicarbonate of soda, egg and milk to the bulk of the mixture and beat until smooth. Spoon the main mixture into a greased and floured 20 cm/8 in microwave dish and sprinkle the nut mixture over the top. Microwave on High for 8 minutes. Leave to cool in the dish for 10 minutes and serve warm.

Microwave Orange Juice Cake

Makes one 20 cm/8 in cake

250 g/9 oz/2¼ cups plain (all-purpose) flour

225 g/8 oz/1 cup granulated sugar

15 ml/1 tbsp baking powder

2.5 ml/½ tsp salt

60 ml/4 tbsp oil

250 ml/8 fl oz/2 cups orange juice

2 eggs, separated

100 g/4 oz/½ cup caster (superfine) sugar

Orange Butter Icing

Orange Glacé Icing

Mix together the flour, granulated sugar, baking powder, salt, oil and half the orange juice and beat until well blended. Beat in the egg yolks and remaining orange juice until light and soft. Whisk the egg whites until stiff, then add half the caster sugar and beat until thick and glossy. Fold in the remaining sugar, then fold the egg whites into the cake mixture. Spoon into two greased and floured 20 cm/8 in microwave dishes and microwave each one separately on High for 6–8 minutes. Remove from the oven, cover with foil and leave to cool for 5 minutes, then turn out on to a wire rack to finish cooling. Sandwich the cakes together with orange butter icing (frosting) and spread the orange glacé icing over the top.

Microwave Pavlova

Makes one 23 cm/9 in cake

4 egg whites

225 g/8 oz/1 cup caster (superfine) sugar

2.5 ml/½ tsp vanilla essence (extract)

A few drops of wine vinegar

150 ml/¼ pt/2/3 cup whipping cream

1 kiwi fruit, sliced

100 g/4 oz strawberries, sliced

Beat the egg whites until they form soft peaks. Sprinkle in half the sugar and beat well. Gradually add the rest of the sugar, the vanilla essence and vinegar and beat until dissolved. Spoon the mixture into to a 23 cm/9 in circle on a piece of baking parchment. Microwave on High for 2 minutes. Leave to stand in the microwave with the door open for 10 minutes. Remove from the oven, tear off the backing paper and leave to cool. Whip the cream until stiff and spread over the top of the meringue. Arrange the fruit attractively on top.

Microwave Shortcake

Makes one 20 cm/8 in cake

225 g/8 oz/2 cups plain (all-purpose) flour

15 ml/1 tbsp baking powder

50 g/2 oz/¼ cup caster (superfine) sugar

100 g/4 oz/½ cup butter or margarine

75 ml/5 tbsp single (light) cream

1 egg

Mix together the flour, baking powder and sugar, then rub in the butter or margarine until the mixture resembles breadcrumbs. Mix together the cream and egg, then work into the flour mixture until you have a soft dough. Press into a greased 20 cm/8 in microwave dish and microwave on High for 6 minutes. Leave to stand for 4 minutes, then turn out and finish cooling on a wire rack.

Microwave Strawberry Shortcake

Makes one 20 cm/8 in cake

900 g/2 lb strawberries, thickly sliced

225 g/8 oz/1 cup caster (superfine) sugar

225 g/8 oz/2 cups plain (all-purpose) flour

15 ml/1 tbsp baking powder

175 g/6 oz/¾ cup butter or margarine

75 ml/5 tbsp single (light) cream

1 egg

150 ml/¼ pt/2/3 cup double (heavy) cream, whipped

Mix the strawberries with 175 g/ 6 oz/¾ cup of the sugar, then chill for at least 1 hour.

Mix together the flour, baking powder and remaining sugar, then rub in 100 g/ 4 oz/½ cup of the butter or margarine until the mixture resembles breadcrumbs. Mix together the single cream and egg, then work into the flour mixture until you have a soft dough. Press into a greased 20 cm/8 in microwave dish and microwave on High for 6 minutes. Leave to stand for 4 minutes, then turn out and split through the centre while still warm. Leave to cool.

Spread both cut surfaces with the remaining butter or margarine. Spread one-third of the whipped cream over the base, then cover with three-quarters of the strawberries. Top with a further one-third of the cream, then place the second shortcake on top. Top with the remaining cream and strawberries.

Microwave Sponge Cake

Makes one 18 cm/7 in cake

150 g/5 oz/1¼ cups self-raising (self-rising) flour

100 g/4 oz/½ cup butter or margarine

100 g/4 oz/½ cup caster (superfine) sugar

2 eggs

30 ml/2 tbsp milk

Beat together all the ingredients until smooth. Spoon into a base-lined 18 cm/7 in microwave dish and microwave on Medium for 6 minutes. Leave to cool in the dish for 5 minutes, then turn out on to a wire rack to finish cooling.

Microwave Sultana Bars

Makes 12

175 g/6 oz/¾ cup butter or margarine

100 g/4 oz/½ cup caster (superfine) sugar

15 ml/1 tbsp golden (light corn) syrup

75 g/3 oz/½ cup sultanas (golden raisins)

5 ml/1 tsp grated lemon rind

225 g/8 oz/2 cups self-raising (self-rising) flour

For the icing (frosting):

175 g/6 oz/1 cup icing (confectioners') sugar

30 ml/2 tbsp lemon juice

Microwave the butter or margarine, caster sugar and syrup on Medium for 2 minutes. Stir in the sultanas and lemon rind. Fold in the flour. Spoon into a greased and lined 20 cm/8 in square microwave dish and microwave on Medium for 8 minutes until just firm. Leave to cool slightly.

Place the icing sugar in a bowl and make a well in the centre. Gradually mix in the lemon juice to make a smooth icing. Spread over the cake while still just warm, then leave to cool completely.

Microwave Chocolate Biscuits

Makes 24

225 g/8 oz/1 cup butter or margarine, softened

100 g/4 oz/½ cup dark brown sugar

5 ml/1 tsp vanilla essence (extract)

225 g/8 oz/2 cups self-raising (self-rising) flour

50 g/2 oz/½ cup drinking chocolate powder

Cream together the butter, sugar and vanilla essence until light and fluffy. Gradually mix in the flour and chocolate and mix to a smooth dough. Shape into walnut-sized balls, arrange six at a time on a greased microwave baking (cookie) sheet and flatten slightly with a fork. Microwave each batch on High for 2 minutes, until all the biscuits (cookies) are cooked. Leave to cool on a wire rack.

Microwave Coconut Cookies

Makes 24

50 g/2 oz/¼ cup butter or margarine, softened

75 g/3 oz/1/3 cup caster (superfine) sugar

1 egg, lightly beaten

2.5 ml/½ tsp vanilla essence (extract)

75 g/3 oz/¾ cup plain (all-purpose) flour

25 g/1 oz/¼ cup desiccated (shredded) coconut

A pinch of salt

30 ml/2 tbsp strawberry jam (conserve)

Beat together the butter or margarine and sugar until light and fluffy. Stir in the egg and vanilla essence alternately with the flour, coconut and salt and mix to a smooth dough. Shape into walnut-sized balls and arrange six at a time on a greased microwave baking (cookie) sheet, then press lightly with a fork to flatten slightly. Microwave on High for 3 minutes until just firm. Transfer to a wire rack and place a spoonful of jam on the centre of each cookie. Repeat with the remaining cookies.

Microwave Florentines

Makes 12

50 g/2 oz/¼ cup butter or margarine

50 g/2 oz/¼ cup demerara sugar

15 ml/1 tbsp golden (light corn) syrup

50 g/2 oz/¼ cup glacé (candied) cherries

75 g/3 oz/¾ cup walnuts, chopped

25 g/1 oz/3 tbsp sultanas (golden raisins)

25 g/1 oz/¼ cup flaked (slivered) almonds

30 ml/2 tbsp chopped mixed (candied) peel

25 g/1 oz/¼ cup plain (all-purpose) flour

100 g/4 oz/1 cup plain (semi-sweet) chocolate, broken up (optional)

Microwave the butter or margarine, sugar and syrup on High for 1 minute until melted. Stir in the cherries, walnuts, sultanas and almonds, then mix in the mixed peel and flour. Place teaspoonfuls of the mixture, well apart, on greaseproof (waxed) paper and cook four at a time on High for 1½ minutes each batch. Neaten the edges with a knife, leave to cool on the paper for 3 minutes, then transfer to a wire rack to finish cooling. Repeat with the remaining biscuits. If liked, melt the chocolate in a bowl for 30 seconds and spread over one side of the florentines, then leave to set.

Microwave Hazelnut and Cherry Biscuits

Makes 24

100 g/4 oz/½ cup butter or margarine, softened

100 g/4 oz/½ cup caster (superfine) sugar

1 egg, beaten

175 g/6 oz/1½ cups plain (all-purpose) flour

50 g/2 oz/½ cup ground hazelnuts

100 g/4 oz/½ cup glacé (candied) cherries

Cream together the butter or margarine and sugar until light and fluffy. Gradually beat in the egg, then fold in the flour, hazelnuts and cherries. Place spoonfuls well spaced out on microwave baking (cookie) sheets and microwave eight biscuits (cookies) at a time on High for about 2 minutes until just firm.

Microwave Sultana Biscuits

Makes 24

225 g/8 oz/2 cups plain (all-purpose) flour

5 ml/1 tsp ground mixed (apple-pie) spice

175 g/6 oz/¾ cup butter or margarine, softened

100 g/4 oz/2/3 cup sultanas (golden raisins)

175 g/6 oz/¾ cup demerara sugar

Mix together the flour and mixed spice, then blend in the butter or margarine, sultanas and 100 g/4 oz/½ cup of the sugar to make a soft dough. Roll into two sausage shapes about 18 cm/7 in long and roll in the remaining sugar. Cut into slices and arrange six at a time on a greased microwave baking (cookie) sheet and microwave on High for 2 minutes. Leave to cool on a wire rack and repeat with the remaining biscuits (cookies).

Microwave Banana Bread

Makes one 450 g/1 lb loaf

75 g/3 oz/1/3 cup butter or margarine, softened

175 g/6 oz/¾ cup caster (superfine) sugar

2 eggs, lightly beaten

200 g/7 oz/1¾ cups plain (all-purpose) flour

10 ml/2 tsp baking powder

2.5 ml/½ tsp bicarbonate of soda (baking soda)

A pinch of salt

2 ripe bananas

15 ml/1 tbsp lemon juice

60 ml/4 tbsp milk

50 g/2 oz/½ cup walnuts, chopped

Cream together the butter or margarine and sugar until light and fluffy. Gradually beat in the eggs, then fold in the flour, baking powder, bicarbonate of soda and salt. Mash the bananas with the lemon juice, then fold into the mixture with the milk and walnuts. Spoon into a greased and floured 450 g/1 lb microwave loaf tin (pan) and microwave on High for 12 minutes. Remove from the oven, cover with foil and leave to cool for 10 minutes, then turn out on to a wire rack to finish cooling.

Microwave Cheese Bread

Makes one 450 g/1 lb loaf

50 g/2 oz/¼ cup butter or margarine

250 ml/8 fl oz/1 cup milk

2 eggs, lightly beaten

225 g/8 oz/2 cups plain (all-purpose) flour

10 ml/2 tsp baking powder

10 ml/2 tsp mustard powder

2.5 ml/½ tsp salt

175 g/6 oz/1½ cups Cheddar cheese, grated

Melt the butter or margarine in a small bowl on High for 1 minute. Stir in the milk and eggs. Mix together the flour, baking powder, mustard, salt and 100 g/4 oz/1 cup of the cheese. Stir in the milk mixture until well blended. Spoon into a microwave loaf tin (pan) and microwave on High for 9 minutes. Sprinkle with the remaining cheese, cover with foil and leave to stand for 20 minutes.

Microwave Walnut Loaf

Makes one 450 g/1 lb loaf

225 g/8 oz/2 cups plain (all-purpose) flour

300 g/10 oz/1¼ cups caster (superfine) sugar

5 ml/1 tsp baking powder

A pinch of salt

100 g/4 oz/½ cup butter or margarine, softened

150 ml/¼ pt/2/3 cup milk

2.5 ml/½ tsp vanilla essence (extract)

4 egg whites

50 g/2 oz/½ cup walnuts, chopped

Mix together the flour, sugar, baking powder and salt. Beat in the butter or margarine, then the milk and vanilla essence. Beat in the egg whites until creamy, then fold in the nuts. Spoon into a greased and floured 450 g/1 lb microwave loaf tin (pan) and microwave on High for 12 minutes. Remove from the oven, cover with foil and leave to cool for 10 minutes, then turn out on to a wire rack to finish cooling.

No-bake Amaretti Cake

Makes one 20 cm/8 in cake

100 g/4 oz/½ cup butter or margarine

175 g/6 oz/1½ cups plain (semi-sweet) chocolate

75 g/3 oz Amaretti biscuits (cookies), coarsely crushed

175 g/6 oz/1½ cups walnuts, chopped

50 g/2 oz/½ cup pine nuts

75 g/3 oz/1/3 cup glacé (candied) cherries, chopped

30 ml/2 tbsp Grand Marnier

225 g/8 oz/1 cup Mascarpone cheese

Melt the butter or margarine and chocolate in a heatproof bowl set over a pan of gently simmering water. Remove from the heat and stir in the biscuits, nuts and cherries. Spoon into a sandwich tin (pan) lined with clingfilm (plastic wrap) and press down gently. Chill for 1 hour until set. Turn out on to a serving plate and remove the clingfilm. Beat the Grand Marnier into the Mascarpone and spoon over the base.

American Crispy Rice Bars

Makes about 24 bars

50 g/2 oz/¼ cup butter or margarine

225 g/8 oz white marshmallows

5 ml/1 tsp vanilla essence (extract)

150 g/5 oz/5 cups puffed rice cereal

Melt the butter or margarine in a large pan over a low heat. Add the marshmallows and cook, stirring continuously, until the marshmallows have melted and the mixture is syrupy. Remove from the heat and add the vanilla essence. Stir in the rice cereal until evenly coated. Press into a 23 cm/9 in square tin (pan) and cut into bars. Leave to set.

Apricot Squares

Makes 12

50 g/2 oz/¼ cup butter or margarine

175 g/6 oz/1 small can evaporated milk

15 ml/1 tbsp clear honey

45 ml/3 tbsp apple juice

50 g/2 oz/¼ cup soft brown sugar

50 g/2 oz/1/3 cup sultanas (golden raisins)

225 g/8 oz/11/3 cups ready-to-eat dried apricots, chopped

100 g/4 oz/1 cup desiccated (shredded) coconut

225 g/8 oz/2 cups rolled oats

Melt the butter or margarine with the milk, honey, apple juice and sugar. Stir in the remaining ingredients. Press into a greased 25 cm/12 in baking tin (pan) and chill before cutting into squares.

Apricot Swiss Roll Cake

Makes one 23 cm/9 in cake

400 g/14 oz/1 large can apricot halves, drained and juice reserved

50 g/2 oz/½ cup custard powder

75 g/3 oz/¼ cup apricot jelly (clear conserve)

75 g/3 oz/½ cup ready-to-eat dried apricots, chopped

400 g/14 oz/1 large can condensed milk

225 g/8 oz/1 cup cottage cheese

45 ml/3 tbsp lemon juice

1 Swiss Roll, sliced

Make up the apricot juice with water to make 500 ml/17 fl oz/2¼ cups. Mix the custard powder to a paste with a little of the liquid, then bring the remainder to the boil. Stir in the custard paste and apricot jelly and simmer until thick and shiny, stirring continuously. Mash the canned apricots and add to the mixture with the dried apricots. Leave to cool, stirring occasionally.

Beat together the condensed milk, cottage cheese and lemon juice until well blended, then stir into the jelly mixture. Line a 23 cm/9 in cake tin (pan) with clingfilm (plastic wrap) and arrange the Swiss (jelly) roll slices over the base and sides of the tin. Spoon in the cake mixture and chill until set. Turn out carefully when ready to serve.

Broken Biscuit Cakes

Makes 12

100 g/4 oz/½ cup butter or margarine

30 ml/2 tbsp caster (superfine) sugar

15 ml/1 tbsp golden (light corn) syrup

30 ml/2 tbsp cocoa (unsweetened chocolate) powder

225 g/8 oz/2 cups broken biscuit (cookie) crumbs

50 g/2 oz/1/3 cup sultanas (golden raisins)

Melt the butter or margarine with the sugar and syrup without allowing the mixture to boil. Stir in the cocoa, biscuits and sultanas. Press into a greased 25 cm/10 in baking tin (pan), leave to cool, then chill until firm. Cut into squares.

No-bake Buttermilk Cake

Makes one 23 cm/9 in cake

30 ml/2 tbsp custard powder

100 g/4 oz/½ cup caster (superfine) sugar

450 ml/¾ pt/2 cups milk

175 ml/6 fl oz/¾ cup buttermilk

25 g/1 oz/2 tbsp butter or margarine

400 g/12 oz plain biscuits (cookies), crushed

120 ml/4 fl oz/½ cup whipping cream

Blend the custard powder and sugar to a paste with a little of the milk. Bring the remaining milk to the boil. Stir it into the paste, then return the whole mixture to the pan and stir over a low heat for about 5 minutes until thickened. Stir in the buttermilk and butter or margarine. Spoon layers of crushed biscuits and custard mixture into a 23 cm/9 in cake tin (pan) lined with clingfilm (plastic wrap), or into a glass dish. Press down gently and chill until set. Whip the cream until stiff, then pipe rosettes of cream on the top of the cake. Either serve from the dish, or lift out carefully to serve.

Chestnut Slice

Makes one 900 g/2 lb loaf

225 g/8 oz/2 cups plain (semi-sweet) chocolate

100 g/4 oz/½ cup butter or margarine, softened

100 g/4 oz/½ cup caster (superfine) sugar

450 g/1 lb/1 large can unsweetened chestnut purée

25 g/1 oz/¼ cup rice flour

A few drops of vanilla essence (extract)

150 ml/¼ pt/2/3 cup whipping cream, whipped

Grated chocolate to decorate

Melt the plain chocolate in a heatproof bowl over a pan of gently simmering water. Cream together the butter or margarine and sugar until light and fluffy. Beat in the chestnut purée, chocolate, rice flour and vanilla essence. Turn into a greased and lined 900 g/2 lb loaf tin (pan) and chill until firm. Decorate with whipped cream and grated chocolate before serving.

Chestnut Sponge Cake

Makes one 900 g/2 lb cake

For the cake:

400 g/14 oz/1 large can sweetened chestnut purée

100 g/4 oz/½ cup butter or margarine, softened

1 egg

A few drops of vanilla essence (extract)

30 ml/2 tbsp brandy

24 sponge finger biscuits (cookies)

For the glaze:

30 ml/2 tbsp cocoa (unsweetened chocolate) powder

15 ml/1 tbsp caster (superfine) sugar

30 ml/2 tbsp water

For the butter cream:

100 g/4 oz/½ cup butter or margarine, softened

100 g/4 oz/2/3 cup icing (confectioners') sugar, sifted

15 ml/1 tbsp coffee essence (extract)

To make the cake, blend together the chestnut purée, butter or margarine, egg, vanilla essence and 15 ml/1 tbsp of the brandy and beat until smooth. Grease and line a 900 g/2 lb loaf tin (pan) and line the base and sides with the sponge fingers. Sprinkle the remaining brandy over the biscuits and spoon the chestnut mixture into the centre. Chill until firm.

Lift out of the tin and remove the lining paper. Dissolve the glaze ingredients in a heatproof bowl set over a pan of gently simmering water, stirring until smooth. Leave to cool slightly, then brush most of the glaze over the top of the cake. Cream together the butter cream ingredients until smooth, then pipe into swirls around the edge of the cake. Drizzle with the reserved glaze to finish.

Chocolate and Almond Bars

Makes 12

175 g/6 oz/1½ cups plain (semi-sweet) chocolate, chopped

3 eggs, separated

120 ml/4 fl oz/½ cup milk

10 ml/2 tsp powdered gelatine

120 ml/4 fl oz/½ cup double (heavy) cream

45 ml/3 tbsp caster (superfine) sugar

60 ml/4 tbsp flaked (slivered) almonds, toasted

Melt the chocolate in a heatproof bowl set over a pan of gently simmering water. Remove from the heat and beat in the egg yolks. Boil the milk in a separate pan, then whisk in the gelatine. Stir into the chocolate mixture, then stir in the cream. Beat the egg whites until stiff, then add the sugar and beat again until stiff and glossy. Fold into the mixture. Spoon into a greased and lined 450 g/1 lb loaf tin (pan), sprinkle with the toasted almonds and leave to cool, then chill for at least 3 hours until set. Turn over and cut into thick slices to serve

Chocolate Crisp Cake

Makes one 450 g/1 lb loaf

150 g/5 oz/2/3 cup butter or margarine
30 ml/2 tbsp golden (light corn) syrup

175 g/6 oz/1½ cups digestive biscuit (Graham cracker) crumbs

50 g/2 oz/2 cups puffed rice cereal

25 g/1 oz/3 tbsp sultanas (golden raisins)

25 g/1 oz/2 tbsp glacé (candied) cherries, chopped

225 g/8 oz/2 cups chocolate chips

30 ml/2 tbsp water

175 g/6 oz/1 cup icing (confectioners') sugar, sifted

Melt 100 g/4 oz/½ cup of the butter or margarine with the syrup, then remove from the heat and stir in the biscuit crumbs, cereal, sultanas, cherries and three-quarters of the chocolate chips. Spoon into a greased and lined 450 g/1 lb loaf tin (pan) and smooth the top. Chill until firm. Melt the remaining butter or margarine with the remaining chocolate and the water. Stir in the icing sugar and mix until smooth. Remove the cake from the tin and halve lengthways. Sandwich together with half the chocolate icing (frosting), place on a serving plate, then pour over the remaining icing. Chill before serving.

Chocolate Crumb Squares

Makes about 24

225 g/8 oz digestive biscuits (Graham crackers)

100 g/4 oz/½ cup butter or margarine

25 g/1 oz/2 tbsp caster (superfine) sugar

15 ml/1 tbsp golden (light corn) syrup

45 ml/3 tbsp cocoa (unsweetened chocolate) powder

200 g/7 oz/1¾ cups chocolate cake covering

Place the biscuits in a plastic bag and crush with a rolling pin. Melt the butter or margarine in a pan, then stir in the sugar and syrup. Remove from the heat and stir in the biscuit crumbs and cocoa. Turn into a greased and lined 18 cm/7 in square cake tin and press down evenly. Leave to cool, then chill in the fridge until set.

Melt the chocolate in a heatproof bowl set over a pan of gently simmering water. Spread over the biscuit, marking into lines with a fork while setting. Cut into squares when firm.

Chocolate Fridge Cake

Makes one 450 g/1 lb cake

100 g/4 oz/½ cup soft brown sugar

100 g/4 oz/½ cup butter or margarine

50 g/2 oz/½ cup drinking chocolate powder

25 g/1 oz/¼ cup cocoa (unsweetened chocolate) powder

30 ml/2 tbsp golden (light corn) syrup

150 g/5 oz digestive biscuits (Graham crackers) or rich tea biscuits

50 g/2 oz/¼ cup glacé (candied) cherries or mixed nuts and raisins

100 g/4 oz/1 cup milk chocolate

Place the sugar, butter or margarine, drinking chocolate, cocoa and syrup in a pan and warm gently until the butter has melted, stirring well. Remove from the heat and crumble in the biscuits. Stir in the cherries or nuts and raisins and spoon into a 450 g/1 lb loaf tin (pan). Leave in the fridge to cool.

Melt the chocolate in a heatproof bowl over a pan of gently simmering water. Spread over the top of the cooled cake and slice when set.

Chocolate and Fruit Cake

Makes one 18 cm/7 in cake

100 g/4 oz/½ cup butter or margarine, melted

100 g/4 oz/½ cup soft brown sugar

225 g/8 oz/2 cups digestive biscuit (Graham cracker) crumbs

50 g/2 oz/1/3 cup sultanas (golden raisins)

45 ml/3 tbsp cocoa (unsweetened chocolate) powder

1 egg, beaten

A few drops of vanilla essence (extract)

Mix the butter or margarine and sugar, then stir in the remaining ingredients and beat well. Spoon into a greased 18 cm/7 in sandwich tin (pan) and smooth the surface. Chill until set.

Chocolate and Ginger Squares

Makes 24

100 g/4 oz/½ cup butter or margarine

100 g/4 oz/½ cup soft brown sugar

30 ml/2 tbsp cocoa (unsweetened chocolate) powder

1 egg, lightly beaten

225 g/8 oz/2 cups ginger biscuit (cookie) crumbs

15 ml/1 tbsp chopped crystallised (candied) ginger

Melt the butter or margarine, then stir in the sugar and cocoa until well blended. Mix in the egg, biscuit crumbs and ginger. Press into a Swiss roll tin (jelly roll pan) and chill until firm. Cut into squares.

Luxury Chocolate and Ginger Squares

Makes 24

100 g/4 oz/½ cup butter or margarine

100 g/4 oz/½ cup soft brown sugar

30 ml/2 tbsp cocoa (unsweetened chocolate) powder

1 egg, lightly beaten

225 g/8 oz/2 cups ginger biscuit (cookie) crumbs

15 ml/1 tbsp chopped crystallised (candied) ginger

100 g/4 oz/1 cup plain (semi-sweet) chocolate

Melt the butter or margarine, then stir in the sugar and cocoa until well blended. Mix in the egg, biscuit crumbs and ginger. Press into a Swiss roll tin (jelly roll pan) and chill until firm.

> Melt the chocolate in a heatproof bowl set over a pan of gently simmering water. Spread over the cake and leave to set. Cut into squares when the chocolate is almost hard.

Honey Chocolate Cookies

Makes 12

225 g/8 oz/1 cup butter or margarine

30 ml/2 tbsp clear honey

90 ml/6 tbsp carob or cocoa (unsweetened chocolate) powder

225 g/8 oz/2 cups sweet biscuit (cookie) crumbs

Melt the butter or margarine, honey and carob or cocoa powder in a pan until well blended. Mix in the biscuit crumbs. Spoon into a greased 20 cm/8 in square cake tin (pan) and leave to cool, then cut into squares.

Chocolate Layer Cake

Makes one 450 g/1 lb cake

300 ml/½ pt/1¼ cups double (heavy) cream

225 g/8 oz/2 cups plain (semi-sweet) chocolate, broken up

5 ml/1 tsp vanilla essence (extract)

20 plain biscuits (cookies)

Heat the cream in a pan over a low heat until almost boiling. Remove from the heat and add the chocolate, stir, cover and leave for 5 minutes. Stir in the vanilla essence and mix until well blended, then chill until the mixture begins to thicken.

Line a 450g /1 lb loaf tin (pan) with clingfilm (plastic wrap). Spread a layer of chocolate on the bottom, then arrange a few biscuits in a layer on top. Continue layering the chocolate and biscuits until you have used them up. Finish with a layer of chocolate. Cover with clingfilm and chill for at least 3 hours. Turn out the cake and remove the clingfilm.

Nice Chocolate Bars

Makes 12

100 g/4 oz/½ cup butter or margarine

30 ml/2 tbsp golden (light corn) syrup

30 ml/2 tbsp cocoa (unsweetened chocolate) powder

225 g/8 oz/1 packet Nice or plain biscuits (cookies), roughly crushed

100 g/4 oz/1 cup plain (semi-sweet) chocolate, diced

Melt the butter or margarine and syrup, then remove from the heat and stir in the cocoa and crushed biscuits. Spread the mixture in a 23 cm/9 in square cake tin (pan) and level the surface. Melt the chocolate in a heatproof bowl over a pan of gently simmering water and spread over the top. Leave to cool slightly, then cut into bars or squares and chill until set.

Chocolate Praline Squares

Makes 12

100 g/4 oz/½ cup butter or margarine

30 ml/2 tbsp caster (superfine) sugar

15 ml/1 tbsp golden (light corn) syrup

15 ml/1 tbsp drinking chocolate powder

225 g/8 oz digestive biscuits (Graham crackers), crushed

200 g/7 oz/1¾ cups plain (semi-sweet) chocolate

100 g/4 oz/1 cup chopped mixed nuts

Melt the butter or margarine, sugar, syrup and drinking chocolate in a pan. Bring to the boil, then boil for 40 seconds. Remove from the heat and stir in the biscuits and nuts. Press into a greased 28 x 18 cm/11 x 7 in cake tin (pan). Melt the chocolate in a heatproof bowl over a pan of gently simmering water. Spread over the biscuits and leave to cool, then chill for 2 hours before cutting into squares.

Coconut Crunchies

Makes 12

100 g/4 oz/1 cup plain (semi-sweet) chocolate

30 ml/2 tbsp milk

30 ml/2 tbsp golden (light corn) syrup

100 g/4 oz/4 cups puffed rice cereal

50 g/2 oz/½ cup desiccated (shredded) coconut

Melt the chocolate, milk and syrup in a pan. Remove from the heat and stir in the cereal and coconut. Spoon into paper cake cases (cupcake papers) and leave to set.

Crunch Bars

Makes 12

175 g/6 oz/¾ cup butter or margarine

50 g/2 oz/¼ cup soft brown sugar

30 ml/2 tbsp golden (light corn) syrup

45 ml/3 tbsp cocoa (unsweetened chocolate) powder

75 g/3 oz/½ cup raisins or sultanas (golden raisins)

350 g/12 oz/3 cups oat crunch cereal

225 g/8 oz/2 cups plain (semi-sweet) chocolate

Melt the butter or margarine with the sugar, syrup and cocoa. Stir in the raisins or sultanas and the cereal. Press the mixture into a greased 25 cm/12 in baking tin (pan). Melt the chocolate in a heatproof bowl over a pan of gently simmering water. Spread over the bars and leave to cool, then chill before cutting into bars.

Coconut and Raisin Crunchies

Makes 12

100 g/4 oz/1 cup white chocolate

30 ml/2 tbsp milk

30 ml/2 tbsp golden (light corn) syrup

175 g/6 oz/6 cups puffed rice cereal

50 g/2 oz/1/3 cup raisins

Melt the chocolate, milk and syrup in a pan. Remove from the heat and stir in the cereal and raisins. Spoon into paper cake cases (cupcake papers) and leave to set.

Coffee Milk Squares

Makes 20

25 g/1 oz/2 tbsp powdered gelatine

75 ml/5 tbsp cold water

225 g/8 oz/2 cups plain biscuit (cookie) crumbs

50 g/2 oz/¼ cup butter or margarine, melted

400 g/14 oz/1 large can evaporated milk

150 g/5 oz/2/3 cup caster (superfine) sugar

400 ml/14 fl oz/1¾ cups strong black coffee, ice cold

Whipped cream and crystallised (candied) orange slices to decorate

Sprinkle the gelatine over the water in a bowl and leave until spongy. Stand the bowl in a pan of hot water and leave until dissolved. Leave to cool slightly. Stir the biscuit crumbs into the melted butter and press into the base and sides of a greased 30 x 20 cm/12 x 8 in rectangular cake tin (pan). Beat the evaporated milk until thick, then gradually beat in the sugar, followed by the dissolved gelatine and the coffee. Spoon over the base and chill until set. Cut into squares and decorate with piped whipped cream and crystallised (candied) orange slices.

No-bake Fruit Cake

Makes one 23 cm/9 in cake

450 g/1 lb/22/3 cups dried mixed fruit (fruit cake mix)

450 g/1 lb plain biscuits (cookies), crushed

100 g/4 oz/½ cup butter or margarine, melted

100 g/4 oz/½ cup soft brown sugar

400 g/14 oz/1 large can condensed milk

5 ml/1 tsp vanilla essence (extract)

Mix together all the ingredients until well blended. Spoon into a greased 23 cm/9 in cake tin (pan) lined with clingfilm (plastic wrap) and press down. Chill until firm.

Fruity Squares

Makes about 12

100 g/4 oz/½ cup butter or margarine

100 g/4 oz/½ cup soft brown sugar

400 g/14 oz/1 large can condensed milk

5 ml/1 tsp vanilla essence (extract)

250 g/9 oz/1½ cups dried mixed fruit (fruit cake mix)

100 g/4 oz/½ cup glacé (candied) cherries

50 g/2 oz/½ cup chopped mixed nuts

400 g/14 oz plain biscuits (cookies), crushed

Melt the butter or margarine and sugar over a low heat. Stir in the condensed milk and vanilla essence and remove from the heat. Mix in the remaining ingredients. Press into a greased Swiss roll tin (jelly roll pan) and chill for 24 hours until firm. Cut into squares.

Fruit and Fibre Crackles

Makes 12

100 g/4 oz/1 cup plain (semi-sweet) chocolate

50 g/2 oz/¼ cup butter or margarine

15 ml/1 tbsp golden (light corn) syrup

100 g/4 oz/1 cup fruit and fibre breakfast cereal

Melt the chocolate in a heatproof bowl over a pan of gently simmering water. Beat in the butter or margarine and syrup. Stir in the cereal. Spoon into paper cake cases (cupcake papers) and leave to cool and set.

Nougat Layer Cake

Makes one 900 g/2 lb cake

15 g/½ oz/1 tbsp powdered gelatine

100 ml/3½ fl oz/6½ tbsp water

1 packet trifle sponges

225 g/8 oz/1 cup butter or margarine, softened

50 g/2 oz/¼ cup caster (superfine) sugar

400 g/14 oz/1 large can condensed milk

5 ml/1 tsp lemon juice

5 ml/1 tsp vanilla essence (extract)

5 ml/1 tsp cream of tartar

100 g/4 oz/2/3 cup dried mixed fruit (fruit cake mix), chopped

Sprinkle the gelatine over the water in a small bowl, then stand the bowl in a pan of hot water until the gelatine is transparent. Cool slightly. Line a 900 g/2 lb loaf tin (pan) with foil so that the foil will cover the top of the tin, then arrange half the trifle sponges on the base. Beat together the butter or margarine and sugar until creamy, then beat in all the remaining ingredients. Spoon into the tin and arrange the remaining trifle sponges on top. Cover with foil and put a weight on the top. Chill until firm.

Milk and Nutmeg Squares

Makes 20

For the base:

225 g/8 oz/2 cups plain biscuit (cookie) crumbs

30 ml/2 tbsp soft brown sugar

2.5 ml/½ tsp grated nutmeg

100 g/4 oz/½ cup butter or margarine, melted

For the filling:

1.2 litres/2 pts/5 cups milk

25 g/1 oz/2 tbsp butter or margarine

2 eggs, separated

225 g/8 oz/1 cup caster (superfine) sugar

100 g/4 oz/1 cup cornflour (cornstarch)

50 g/2 oz/½ cup plain (all-purpose) flour

5 ml/1 tsp baking powder

A pinch of grated nutmeg

Grated nutmeg for sprinkling

To make the base, mix the biscuit crumbs, sugar and nutmeg into the melted butter or margarine and press into the base of a greased 30 x 20 cm/12 x 8 in cake tin (pan).

To make the filling, bring 1 litre/ 1¾ pts/4¼ cups of the milk to the boil in a large pan. Add the butter or margarine. Beat the egg yolks with the remaining milk. Mix in the sugar, cornflour, flour, baking powder and nutmeg. Beat a little of the boiling milk into the egg yolk mixture until blended to a paste, then mix the paste into the boiling milk, stirring continuously over a low heat for a few minutes until thickened. Remove from the heat. Beat the egg whites until stiff, then fold them into the mixture. Spoon over the base and sprinkle generously with nutmeg. Leave to cool, then chill and cut into squares before serving.

Muesli Crunch

Makes about 16 squares

400 g/14 oz/3½ cups plain (semi-sweet) chocolate

45 ml/3 tbsp golden (light corn) syrup

25 g/1 oz/2 tbsp butter or margarine

About 225 g/8 oz/2/3 cup muesli

Melt together half the chocolate, the syrup and butter or margarine. Gradually stir in enough muesli to make a stiff mixture. Press into a greased Swiss roll tin (jelly roll pan). Melt the remaining chocolate and smooth over the top. Chill in the fridge before cutting into squares.

Orange Mousse Squares

Makes 20

25 g/1 oz/2 tbsp powdered gelatine

75 ml/5 tbsp cold water

225 g/8 oz/2 cups plain biscuit (cookie) crumbs

50 g/2 oz/¼ cup butter or margarine, melted

400 g/14 oz/1 large can evaporated milk

150 g/5 oz/2/3 cup caster (superfine) sugar

400 ml/14 fl oz/1¾ cups orange juice

Whipped cream and chocolate sweets to decorate

Sprinkle the gelatine over the water in a bowl and leave until spongy. Stand the bowl in a pan of hot water and leave until dissolved. Leave to cool slightly. Stir the biscuit crumbs into the melted butter and press on to the base and sides of a greased 30 x 20 cm/12 x 8 in shallow cake tin (pan). Beat the milk until thick, then gradually beat in the sugar, followed by the dissolved gelatine and the orange juice. Spoon over the base and chill until set. Cut into squares and decorate with piped whipped cream and chocolate sweets.

Peanut Squares

Makes 18

225 g/8 oz/2 cups plain biscuit (cookie) crumbs

100 g/4 oz/½ cup butter or margarine, melted

225 g/8 oz/1 cup crunchy peanut butter

25 g/1 oz/2 tbsp glacé (candied) cherries

25 g/1 oz/3 tbsp currants

Mix together all the ingredients until well blended. Press into a greased 25 cm/12 in baking tin (pan) and chill until firm, then cut into squares.

Peppermint Caramel Cakes

Makes 16

400 g/14 oz/1 large can condensed milk

600 ml/1 pt/2½ cups milk

30 ml/2 tbsp custard powder

225 g/8 oz/2 cups digestive biscuit (Graham cracker) crumbs

100 g/4 oz/1 cup peppermint chocolate, broken into pieces

Place the unopened can of condensed milk in a pan filled with sufficient water to cover the can. Bring to the boil, cover and simmer for 3 hours, topping up with boiling water as necessary. Leave to cool, then open the can and remove the caramel.

Heat 500 ml/17 fl oz/2¼ cups of the milk with the caramel, bring to the boil and stir together until melted. Mix the custard powder to a paste with the remaining milk, then stir it into the pan and continue to simmer until thickened, stirring continuously. Sprinkle half the biscuit crumbs over the base of a greased 20 cm/8 in square cake tin (pan), then spoon half the caramel custard on top and sprinkle with half the chocolate. Repeat the layers, then leave to cool. Chill, then cut into portions to serve.

Rice Cookies

Makes 24

175 g/6 oz/½ cup clear honey

225 g/8 oz/1 cup granulated sugar

60 ml/4 tbsp water

350 g/12 oz/1 box puffed rice cereal

100 g/4 oz/1 cup roasted peanuts

Melt the honey, sugar and water in a large pan, then leave to cool for 5 minutes. Stir in the cereal and peanuts. Roll into balls, place in paper cake cases (cupcake papers) and leave until cool and set.

Rice and Chocolate Toffette

Makes 225 g/8 oz

50 g/2 oz/¼ cup butter or margarine

30 ml/2 tbsp golden (light corn) syrup

30 ml/2 tbsp cocoa (unsweetened chocolate) powder

60 ml/4 tbsp caster (superfine) sugar

50 g/2 oz/½ cup ground rice

Melt the butter and syrup. Stir in the cocoa and sugar until dissolved, then stir in the ground rice. Bring gently to the boil, reduce the heat and simmer gently for 5 minutes, stirring continuously. Spoon into a greased and lined 20 cm/8 in square tin (pan) and leave to cool slightly. Cut into squares, then leave to cool completely before lifting out of the tin.

Almond Paste

Covers the top and sides of one 23 cm/9 in cake

225 g/8 oz/2 cups ground almonds

225 g/8 oz/1 1/3 cups icing (confectioners') sugar, sifted

225 g/8 oz/1 cup caster (superfine) sugar

2 eggs, lightly beaten

10 ml/2 tsp lemon juice

A few drops of almond essence (extract)

Beat together the almonds and sugars. Gradually blend in the remaining ingredients until you have a smooth paste. Wrap in clingfilm (plastic wrap) and chill before use.

Sugar-free Almond Paste

Covers the top and sides of one 15 cm/6 in cake

100 g/4 oz/1 cup ground almonds

50 g/2 oz/½ cup fructose

25 g/1 oz/¼ cup cornflour (cornstarch)

1 egg, lightly beaten

Blend together all the ingredients until you have a smooth paste. Wrap in clingfilm (plastic wrap) and chill before using.

Royal Icing

Covers the top and sides of one 20 cm/8 in cake

5 ml/1 tsp lemon juice

2 egg whites

450 g/1 lb/22/3 cups icing (confectioners') sugar, sifted

5 ml/1 tsp glycerine (optional)

Mix together the lemon juice and egg whites and gradually beat in the icing sugar until the icing (frosting) is smooth and white and will coat the back of a spoon. A few drops of glycerine will prevent the icing from becoming too brittle. Cover with a damp cloth and leave to stand for 20 minutes to allow any air bubbles to rise to the surface.

Icing of this consistency can be poured on to the cake and smoothed with a knife dipped in hot water. For piping, mix in extra icing sugar so that the icing is stiff enough to stand in peaks.

Sugar-free Icing

Makes enough to cover one 15 cm/6 in cake

50 g/2 oz/½ cup fructose

A pinch of salt

1 egg white

2.5 ml/½ tsp lemon juice

Process the fructose powder in a food processor until it is as fine as icing sugar. Blend in the salt. Transfer to a heatproof bowl and whisk in the egg white and lemon juice. Place the bowl over a pan of gently simmering water and continue to whisk until stiff peaks form. Remove from the heat and whisk until cool.

Fondant Icing

Makes enough to cover one 20 cm/8 in cake

450 g/1 lb/2 cups caster (superfine) or lump sugar

150 ml/¼ pt/2/3 cup water

15 ml/1 tbsp liquid glucose or 2.5 ml/½ tsp cream of tartar

Dissolve the sugar in the water in a large, heavy-based pan over a low heat. Wipe down the sides of the pan with a brush dipped in cold water to prevent crystals forming. Dissolve the cream of tartar in a little water, then stir into the pan. Bring to the boil and boil steadily to 115°C/242°F when a drop of icing forms a soft ball when dropped into cold water. Slowly pour the syrup into a heatproof bowl and leave until a skin forms. Beat the icing with a wooden spoon until it becomes opaque and firm. Knead until smooth. Warm in a heatproof bowl over a pan of hot water to soften, if necessary, before use.

Butter Icing

Makes enough to fill and cover one 20 cm/8 in cake

100 g/4 oz/½ cup butter or margarine, softened

225 g/ 8 oz/11/3 cups icing (confectioners') sugar, sifted

30 ml/2 tbsp milk

Beat the butter or margarine until soft. Gradually beat in the icing sugar and milk until well blended.

Chocolate Butter Icing

Makes enough to fill and cover one 20 cm/8 in cake

30 ml/2 tbsp cocoa (unsweetened chocolate) powder

15 ml/1 tbsp boiling water

100 g/4 oz/½ cup butter or margarine, softened

225 g/8 oz/11/3 cups icing (confectioners') sugar, sifted

15 ml/1 tbsp milk

Mix the cocoa to a paste with the boiling water, then leave to cool. Beat the butter or margarine until soft. Gradually beat in the icing sugar, milk and cocoa mixture until well blended.

White Chocolate Butter Icing

Makes enough to fill and cover one 20 cm/8 in cake

100 g/4 oz/1 cup white chocolate

100 g/4 oz/½ cup butter or margarine, softened

225 g/8 oz/11/3 cups icing (confectioners') sugar, sifted

15 ml/1 tbsp milk

Melt the chocolate in a heatproof bowl set over a pan of gently simmering water, then leave to cool slightly. Beat the butter or margarine until soft. Gradually beat in the icing sugar, milk and chocolate until well blended.

Coffee Butter Icing

Makes enough to fill and cover one 20 cm/8 in cake

100 g/4 oz/½ cup butter or margarine, softened

225 g/ 8 oz/1 1/3 cups icing (confectioners') sugar, sifted

15 ml/1 tbsp milk

15 ml/1 tbsp coffee essence (extract)

Beat the butter or margarine until soft. Gradually beat in the icing sugar, milk and coffee essence until well blended.

Lemon Butter Icing

Makes enough to fill and cover one 20 cm/8 in cake

100 g/4 oz/½ cup butter or margarine, softened

225 g/ 8 oz/11/3 cups icing (confectioners') sugar, sifted

30 ml/2 tbsp lemon juice

Grated rind of 1 lemon

Beat the butter or margarine until soft. Gradually beat in the icing sugar, lemon juice and rind until well blended.

Orange Butter Icing

Makes enough to fill and cover one 20 cm/8 in cake

100 g/4 oz/½ cup butter or margarine, softened

225 g/ 8 oz/11/3 cups icing (confectioners') sugar, sifted

30 ml/2 tbsp orange juice

Grated rind of 1 orange

Beat the butter or margarine until soft. Gradually beat in the icing sugar, orange juice and rind until well blended.

Cream Cheese Icing

Makes enough to cover one 25 cm/9 in cake

75 g/3 oz/1/3 cup cream cheese

30 ml/2 tbsp butter or margarine

350 g/12 oz/2 cups icing (confectioners') sugar, sifted

5 ml/1 tsp vanilla essence (extract)

Beat together the cheese and butter or margarine until light and fluffy. Gradually beat in the icing sugar and vanilla essence until you have a smooth, creamy icing.

Orange Icing

Makes enough to cover one 25 cm/9 in cake

250 g/9 oz/1½ cups icing (confectioners') sugar, sifted

30 ml/2 tbsp butter or margarine, softened

A few drops of almond essence (extract)

60 ml/4 tbsp orange juice

Place the icing sugar in a bowl and blend in the butter or margarine and the almond essence. Gradually blend in enough of the orange juice to make a stiff icing.

Orange Liqueur Icing

Makes enough to cover one 20 cm/8 in cake

100 g/4 oz/½ cup butter or margarine, softened

450 g/1 lb/2⅔ cups icing (confectioners') sugar, sifted

60 ml/4 tbsp orange liqueur

15 ml/1 tbsp grated orange rind

Cream together the butter or margarine and sugar until light and fluffy. Beat in enough of the orange liqueur to give a spreadable consistency, then stir in the orange rind.

Peach Cake

Makes one 23 cm/9 in cake

100 g/4 oz/½ cup butter or margarine, softened

225 g/8 oz/1 cup caster (superfine) sugar

3 eggs, separated

450 g/1 lb/4 cups plain (all-purpose) flour

A pinch of salt

5 ml/1 tsp bicarbonate of soda (baking soda)

120 ml/4 fl oz/½ cup milk

225 g/8 oz/2/3 cup peach jam (conserve)

Cream together the butter or margarine and sugar. Gradually beat in the egg yolks, then fold in the flour and salt. Mix the bicarbonate of soda with the milk, then mix into the cake mixture, followed by the jam. Whisk the egg whites until stiff, then fold into the mixture. Spoon in to two greased and lined 23 cm/9 in cake tins (pans) and bake in a preheated oven at 180°C/350°F/gas mark 4 for 25 minutes until well risen and springy to the touch.

Orange and Marsala Cake

Makes one 23 cm/9 in cake

175 g/6 oz/1 cup sultanas (golden raisins)

120 ml/4 fl oz/½ cup Marsala

175 g/6 oz/¾ cup butter or margarine, softened

100 g/4 oz/½ cup soft brown sugar

225 g/8 oz/1 cup caster (superfine) sugar

3 eggs, lightly beaten

Finely grated rind of 1 orange

5 ml/1 tsp orange flower water

275 g/10 oz/2½ cups plain (all-purpose) flour

10 ml/2 tsp bicarbonate of soda (baking soda)

A pinch of salt

375 ml/13 fl oz/1½ cups buttermilk

Orange Liqueur Icing

Soak the sultanas in the Marsala overnight.

Cream together the butter or margarine and sugars until light and fluffy. Gradually beat in the eggs, then mix in the orange rind and orange flower water. Fold in the flour, bicarbonate of soda and salt alternately with the buttermilk. Stir in the soaked sultanas and Marsala. Spoon into two greased and lined 23 cm/9 in cake tins (pans) and bake in a preheated oven at 180°C/350°F/gas mark 4 for 35 minutes until springy to the touch and starting to shrink away from the sides of the tins. Leave to cool in the tins for 10 minutes before turning out on to a wire rack to finish cooling.

Sandwich the cakes together with half the orange liqueur icing, then spread the remaining icing on top.

Peach and Pear Cake

Makes one 23 cm/9 in cake

175 g/6 oz/¾ cup butter or margarine, softened

150 g/5 oz/2/3 cup caster (superfine) sugar

2 eggs, lightly beaten

75 g/3 oz/¾ cup wholemeal (wholewheat) flour

75 g/3 oz/¾ cup plain (all-purpose) flour

10 ml/2 tsp baking powder

15 ml/1 tbsp milk

2 peaches, stoned (pitted), skinned and chopped

2 pears, peeled, cored and chopped

30 ml/2 tbsp icing (confectioners') sugar, sifted

Cream together the butter or margarine and sugar until light and fluffy. Gradually beat in the eggs, then fold in the flours and baking powder, adding the milk to give the mixture a dropping consistency. Fold in the peaches and pears. Spoon the mixture into a greased and lined 23 cm/9 in cake tin (pan) and bake in a preheated oven at 190°C/ 375°F/gas mark 5 for 1 hour until well risen and springy to the touch. Leave to cool in the tin for 10 minutes before turning out on to a wire rack to finish cooling. Dust with icing sugar before serving.

Moist Pineapple Cake

Makes one 20 cm/8 in cake

100 g/4 oz/½ cup butter or margarine

350 g/12 oz/2 cups dried mixed fruit (fruit cake mix)

225 g/8 oz/1 cup soft brown sugar

5 ml/1 tsp ground mixed (apple-pie) spice

5 ml/1 tsp bicarbonate of soda (baking soda)

425 g/15 oz/1 large tin unsweetened crushed pineapple, drained

225 g/8 oz/2 cups self-raising (self-rising) flour

2 eggs, beaten

Place all the ingredients except the flour and eggs in a pan and heat gently to boiling point, stirring well. Boil steadily for 3 minutes, then allow the mixture to cool completely. Stir in the flour, then gradually stir in the eggs. Turn the mixture into a greased and lined 20 cm/8 in cake tin and bake in a preheated oven at 180°C/350°F/gas mark 4 for 1½–1¾ hours until well risen and firm to the touch. Allow to cool in the tin.

Pineapple and Cherry Cake

Makes one 20 cm/8 in cake

100 g/4 oz/½ cup butter or margarine, softened

100 g/4 oz/1 cup caster (superfine) sugar

2 eggs, beaten

225 g/8 oz/2 cups self-raising (self-rising) flour

2.5 ml/½ tsp baking powder

2.5 ml/½ tsp ground cinnamon

175 g/6 oz/1 cup sultanas (golden raisins)

25 g/1 oz/2 tbsp glacé (candied) cherries

400 g/14 oz/1 large can pineapple, drained and chopped

30 ml/2 tbsp brandy or rum

Icing (confectioners') sugar, sifted, for dusting

Cream together the butter or margarine and sugar until light and fluffy. Gradually beat in the eggs, then fold in the flour, baking powder and cinnamon. Gently stir in the remaining ingredients. Spoon the mixture into a greased and lined 20 cm/8 in cake tin (pan) and bake in a preheated oven at 160°C/325°F/ gas mark 3 for 1½ hours until a skewer inserted in the centre comes out clean. Leave to cool, then serve dusted with icing sugar.

Natal Pineapple Cake

Makes one 23 cm/9 in cake

50 g/2 oz/¼ cup butter or margarine

100 g/4 oz/½ cup caster (superfine) sugar

1 egg, lightly beaten

150 g/5 oz/1¼ cups self-raising (self-rising) flour

A pinch of salt

120 ml/4 fl oz/½ cup milk

For the topping:

100 g/4 oz fresh or canned pineapple, coarsely grated

1 eating (dessert) apple, peeled, cored and coarsely grated

120 ml/4 fl oz/½ cup orange juice

15 ml/1 tbsp lemon juice

100 g/4 oz/½ cup caster (superfine) sugar

5 ml/1 tsp ground cinnamon

Melt the butter or margarine, then beat in the sugar and egg until frothy. Stir in the flour and salt alternately with the milk to make a batter. Spoon into a greased and lined 23 cm/9 in cake tin (pan) and bake in a preheated oven at 180°C/350°F/gas mark 4 for 25 minutes until golden and springy.

Bring all the topping ingredients to the boil, then simmer for 10 minutes. Spoon over the warm cake and grill (broil) until the pineapple begins to brown. Cool before serving warm or cold.

Pineapple Upside-down

Makes one 20 cm/8 in cake

175 g/6 oz/¾ cup butter or margarine, softened

175 g/6 oz/¾ cup soft brown sugar

400 g/14 oz/1 large can pineapple slices, drained and juice reserved

4 glacé (candied) cherries, halved

2 eggs

100 g/4 oz/1 cup self-raising (self-rising) flour

Cream 75 g/3 oz/1/3 cup of the butter or margarine with 75 g/3 oz/1/3 cup of the sugar until light and fluffy and spread over the base of a greased 20 cm/8 in cake tin (pan). Arrange the pineapple slices on top and dot with the cherries, rounded-side down. Cream together the remaining butter or margarine and sugar, then gradually beat in the eggs. Fold in the flour and 30 ml/2 tbsp of the reserved pineapple juice. Spoon over the pineapple and bake in a preheated oven at 180°C/350°F/gas mark 4 for 45 minutes until firm to the touch. Leave to cool in the tin for 5 minutes, then carefully remove from the tin and invert on to a wire rack to cool.

Pineapple and Walnut Cake

Makes one 23 cm/9 in cake

225 g/8 oz/1 cup butter or margarine, softened

225 g/8 oz/1 cup caster (superfine) sugar

5 eggs

350 g/12 oz/3 cups plain (all-purpose) flour

100 g/4 oz/1 cup walnuts, coarsely chopped

100 g/4 oz/2/3 cup glacé (candied) pineapple, chopped

A little milk

Cream together the butter or margarine and sugar until light and fluffy. Gradually beat in the eggs, then fold in the flour, nuts and pineapple, adding just enough milk to give a dropping consistency. Spoon into a greased and lined 23 cm/9 in cake tin (pan) and bake in a preheated oven at 150°C/300°F/ gas mark 2 for 1½ hours until a skewer inserted in the centre comes out clean.

Raspberry Cake

Makes one 20 cm/8 in cake

100 g/4 oz/½ cup butter or margarine, softened

200 g/7 oz/scant 1 cup caster (superfine) sugar

2 eggs, lightly beaten

250 ml/8 fl oz/1 cup soured (dairy sour) cream

5 ml/1 tsp vanilla essence (extract)

250 g/9 oz/2¼ cups plain (all-purpose) flour

5 ml/1 tsp baking powder

5 ml/1 tsp bicarbonate of soda (baking soda)

5 ml/1 tsp cocoa (unsweetened chocolate) powder

2.5 ml/½ tsp salt

100 g/4 oz fresh or thawed frozen raspberries

For the topping:

30 ml/2 tbsp caster (superfine) sugar

5 ml/1 tsp ground cinnamon

Cream together the butter or margarine and sugar. Gradually beat in the eggs, then the soured cream and vanilla essence. Fold in the flour, baking powder, bicarbonate of soda, cocoa and salt. Fold in the raspberries. Spoon into a greased 20 cm/8 in cake tin (pan). Mix together the sugar and cinnamon and sprinkle over the top of the cake. Bake in a preheated oven at 200°C/400°F/gas mark 4 for 35 minutes until golden brown and a skewer in the centre comes out clean. Sprinkle with the sugar mixed with the cinnamon.

Rhubarb Cake

Makes one 20 cm/8 in cake

225 g/8 oz/2 cups wholemeal (wholewheat) flour

10 ml/2 tsp baking powder

10 ml/2 tsp ground cinnamon

45 ml/3 tbsp clear honey

175 g/6 oz/1 cup sultanas (golden raisins)

2 eggs

150 ml/¼ pt/2/3 cup milk

225 g/8 oz rhubarb, chopped

30 ml/2 tbsp demerara sugar

Blend all the ingredients except the rhubarb and sugar. Stir in the rhubarb and spoon into a greased and floured 20 cm/8 in cake tin (pan). Sprinkle with the sugar. Bake in a preheated oven at 180°C/350°F/gas mark 4 for 45 minutes until firm. Leave to cool in the tin for 10 minutes before turning out.

Rhubarb-honey Cake

Makes two 450 g/1 lb cakes

250 g/9 oz/2/3 cup clear honey

120 ml/4 fl oz/½ cup oil

1 egg, lightly beaten

15 ml/1 tbsp bicarbonate of soda (baking soda)

150 ml/¼ pt/2/3 cup plain yoghurt

75 ml/5 tbsp water

350 g/12 oz/3 cups plain (all-purpose) flour

10 ml/2 tsp salt

350 g/12 oz rhubarb, finely chopped

5 ml/1 tsp vanilla essence (extract)

50 g/2 oz/½ cup chopped mixed nuts

For the topping:

75 g/3 oz/1/3 cup soft brown sugar

5 ml/1 tsp ground cinnamon

15 ml/1 tbsp butter or margarine, melted

Mix together the honey and oil, then beat in the egg. Mix the bicarbonate of soda into the yoghurt and water until dissolved. Mix the flour and salt and add to the honey mixture alternately with the yoghurt. Stir in the rhubarb, vanilla essence and nuts. Pour into two greased and lined 450 g/1 lb loaf tins (pans). Mix together the topping ingredients and sprinkle over the cakes. Bake in a preheated oven at 160°C/325°F/gas mark 3 for 1 hour until just firm to the touch and golden on top. Leave to cool in the tins for 10 minutes, then turn out on to a wire rack to finish cooling.

Beetroot Cake

Makes one 20 cm/8 in cake

250 g/9 oz/1¼ cups plain (all-purpose) flour

15 ml/1 tbsp baking powder

5 ml/1 tsp ground cinnamon

A pinch of salt

150 ml/8 fl oz/1 cup oil

300 g/11 oz/11/3 cups caster (superfine) sugar

3 eggs, separated

150 g/5 oz raw beetroot, peeled and coarsely grated

150 g/5 oz carrots, coarsely grated

100 g/4 oz/1 cup chopped mixed nuts

Mix together the flour, baking powder, cinnamon and salt. Beat in the oil and sugar. Beat in the eggs yolks, beetroot, carrots and nuts. Whisk the egg whites until stiff, then fold into the mixture using a metal spoon. Spoon the mixture into a greased and lined 20 cm/8 in cake tin (pan) and bake in a preheated oven at 180°C/350°F/gas mark 4 for 1 hour until springy to the touch.

Carrot and Banana Cake

Makes one 20 cm/8 in cake

175 g/6 oz carrots, grated

2 bananas, mashed

75 g/3 oz/½ cup sultanas (golden raisins)

50 g/2 oz/½ cup chopped mixed nuts

175 g/6 oz/1½ cups self-raising (self-rising) flour

5 ml/1 tsp baking powder

5 ml/1 tsp ground mixed (apple-pie) spice

Juice and grated rind of 1 orange

2 eggs, beaten

75 g/3 oz/1/2 cup light muscovado sugar

100 ml/31/2 fl oz/scant 1/2 cup sunflower oil

Mix together all the ingredients until well blended. Spoon into a greased and lined 20 cm/8 in cake tin (pan) and bake in a preheated oven at 180°C/350°F/ gas mark 4 for 1 hour until a skewer inserted in the centre comes out clean.

Carrot and Apple Cake

Makes one 23 cm/9 in cake

250 g/9 oz/2¼ cups self-raising (self-rising) flour

5 ml/1 tsp bicarbonate of soda (baking soda)

5 ml/1 tsp ground cinnamon

175 g/6 oz/¾ cup soft brown sugar

Finely grated rind of 1 orange

3 eggs

200 ml/7 fl oz/scant 1 cup oil

150 g/5 oz eating (dessert) apples, peeled, cored and grated

150 g/5 oz carrots, grated

100 g/4 oz/2/3 cup ready-to-eat dried apricots, chopped

100 g/4 oz/1 cup pecan nuts or walnuts, chopped

Mix together the flour, bicarbonate of soda and cinnamon, then stir in the sugar and orange rind. Beat the eggs into the oil, then stir in the apple, carrots and two-thirds of the apricots and nuts. Fold in the flour mixture and spoon into a greased and lined 23 cm/9 in cake tin (pan). Sprinkle with the remaining chopped apricots and nuts. Bake in a preheated oven at 180°C/350°F/gas mark 4 for 30 minutes until springy to the touch. Leave to cool slightly in the tin, then turn out on to a wire rack to finish cooling.

Carrot and Cinnamon Cake

Makes one 20 cm/8 in cake

100 g/4 oz/1 cup wholemeal (wholewheat) flour

100 g/4 oz/1 cup plain (all-purpose) flour

15 ml/1 tbsp ground cinnamon

5 ml/1 tsp grated nutmeg

10 ml/2 tsp baking powder

100 g/4 oz/½ cup butter or margarine

100 g/4 oz/1/3 cup clear honey

100 g/4 oz/½ cup soft brown sugar

225 g/8 oz carrots, grated

Mix together the flours, cinnamon, nutmeg and baking powder in a bowl. Melt the butter or margarine with the honey and sugar, then mix into the flour. Stir in the carrots and combine well. Spoon into a greased and lined 20 cm/8 in cake tin (pan) and bake in a preheated oven at 160°C/325°F/gas mark 3 for 1 hour until a skewer inserted in the centre comes out clean. Leave to cool in the tin for 10 minutes, then turn out on to a wire rack to finish cooling.

Carrot and Courgette Cake

Makes one 23 cm/9 in cake

2 eggs

175 g/6 oz/¾ cup soft brown sugar

100 g/4 oz carrots, grated

50 g/2 oz courgettes (zucchini), grated

75 ml/5 tbsp oil

225 g/8 oz/2 cups self-raising (self-rising) flour

2.5 ml/½ tsp baking powder

5 ml/1 tsp ground mixed (apple-pie) spice

Cream Cheese Icing

Mix together the eggs, sugar, carrots, courgettes and oil. Stir in the flour, baking powder and mixed spice and mix to a smooth batter. Spoon into a greased and lined 23 cm/9 in cake tin (pan) and bake in a preheated oven at 180°C/350°F/ gas mark 4 for 30 minutes until a skewer inserted in the centre comes out clean. Leave to cool, then spread with cream cheese icing.

Carrot and Ginger Cake

Makes one 20 cm/8 in cake

175 g/6 oz/2/3 cup butter or margarine

100 g/4 oz/1/3 cup golden (light corn) syrup

120 ml/4 fl oz/½ cup water

100 g/4 oz/½ cup soft brown sugar

150 g/5 oz carrots, coarsely grated

5 ml/1 tsp bicarbonate of soda (baking soda)

200 g/7 oz/1¾ cups plain (all-purpose) flour

100 g/4 oz/1 cup self-raising (self-rising) flour

5 ml/1 tsp ground ginger

A pinch of salt

For the icing (frosting):
175 g/6 oz/1 cup icing (confectioners') sugar, sifted

5 ml/1 tsp butter or margarine, softened

30 ml/2 tbsp lemon juice

Melt the butter or margarine with the syrup, water and sugar, then bring to the boil. Remove from the heat and stir in the carrots and bicarbonate of soda. Leave to cool. Mix in the flours, ginger and salt, spoon into a greased 20 cm/8 in cake tin (pan) and bake in a preheated oven at 180°C/350°F/gas mark 4 for 45 minutes until well risen and springy to the touch. Turn out and leave to cool.

Mix the icing sugar with the butter or margarine and enough lemon juice to make a spreadable icing. Cut the cake in half horizontally, then use half the icing to sandwich the cake together and pipe or spread the remainder on top.

Carrot and Nut Cake

Makes one 18 cm/7 in cake

2 large eggs, separated

150 g/5 oz/2/3 cup caster (superfine) sugar

225 g/8 oz carrots, grated

150 g/5 oz/1¼ cups chopped mixed nuts

10 ml/2 tsp grated lemon rind

50 g/2 oz/½ cup plain (all-purpose) flour

2.5 ml/½ tsp baking powder

Whisk together the egg yolks and sugar until thick and creamy. Stir in the carrots, nuts and lemon rind, then fold in the flour and baking powder. Whisk the egg whites until they form soft peaks, then fold into the mixture. Turn into a greased 19 cm/7 in square cake tin (pan). Bake in a preheated oven at 180°C/350°F/gas mark 4 for 40–45 minutes until a skewer inserted into the centre comes out clean.

Carrot, Orange and Nut Cake

Makes one 20 cm/8 in cake

100 g/4 oz/½ cup butter or margarine, softened

100 g/4 oz/½ cup soft brown sugar

5 ml/1 tsp ground cinnamon

5 ml/1 tsp grated orange rind

2 eggs, lightly beaten

15 ml/1 tbsp orange juice

100 g/4 oz carrots, finely grated

50 g/2 oz/½ cup chopped mixed nuts

225 g/8 oz/2 cups self-raising (self-rising) flour

5 ml/1 tsp baking powder

Cream together the butter or margarine, sugar, cinnamon and orange rind until light and fluffy. Gradually beat in the eggs and orange juice, then fold in the carrots, nuts, flour and baking powder. Spoon into a greased and lined 20 cm/8 in cake tin (pan) and bake in a preheated oven at 180°C/350°F/gas mark 4 for 45 minutes until springy to the touch.

Carrot, Pineapple and Coconut Cake

Makes one 25 cm/10 in cake

3 eggs

350 g/12 oz/1½ cups caster (superfine) sugar

300 ml/½ pt/1¼ cups oil

5 ml/1 tsp vanilla essence (extract)

225 g/8 oz/2 cups plain (all-purpose) flour

5 ml/1 tsp bicarbonate of soda (baking soda)

10 ml/2 tsp ground cinnamon

5 ml/1 tsp salt

225 g/8 oz carrots, grated

100 g/4 oz canned pineapple, drained and crushed

100 g/4 oz/1 cup desiccated (shredded) coconut

100 g/4 oz/1 cup chopped mixed nuts

Icing (confectioners') sugar, sifted, for sprinkling

Beat together the eggs, sugar, oil and vanilla essence. Mix together the flour, bicarbonate of soda, cinnamon and salt and gradually beat into the mixture. Fold in the carrots, pineapple, coconut and nuts. Spoon into a greased and floured 25 cm/10 in cake tin (pan) and bake in a preheated oven at 160°C/325°F/gas mark 3 for 1¼ hours until a skewer inserted in the centre comes out clean. Leave to cool in the tin for 10 minutes before turning out on to a wire rack to finish cooling. Sprinkle with icing sugar before serving.

Carrot and Pistachio Cake

Makes one 23 cm/9 in cake

100 g/4 oz/½ cup butter or margarine, softened

100 g/4 oz/½ cup caster (superfine) sugar

2 eggs

225 g/8 oz/2 cups plain (all-purpose) flour

5 ml/1 tsp bicarbonate of soda (baking soda)

5 ml/1 tsp ground cardamom

225 g/8 oz carrots, grated

50 g/2 oz/½ cup pistachio nuts, chopped

50 g/2 oz/½ cup ground almonds

100 g/4 oz/2/3 cup sultanas (golden raisins)

Cream together the butter or margarine and sugar until light and fluffy. Gradually beat in the eggs, beating well after each addition, then fold in the flour, bicarbonate of soda and cardamom. Stir in the carrots, nuts, ground almonds and raisins. Spoon the mixture into a greased and lined 23 cm/9 in cake tin (pan) and bake in a preheated oven at 180°C/ 350°F/gas mark 4 for 40 minutes until well risen, golden and springy to the touch.

Carrot and Walnut Cake

Makes one 23 cm/9 in cake

200 ml/7 fl oz/scant 1 cup oil

4 eggs

225 g/8 oz/2/3 cup clear honey

225 g/8 oz/2 cups wholemeal (wholewheat) flour

10 ml/2 tsp baking powder

2.5 ml/½ tsp bicarbonate of soda (baking soda)

A pinch of salt

5 ml/1 tsp vanilla essence (extract)

175 g/6 oz carrots, coarsely grated

175 g/6 oz/1 cup raisins

100 g/4 oz/1 cup walnuts, finely chopped

Blend together the oil, eggs and honey. Gradually mix in all the remaining ingredients and beat until well blended. Spoon into a greased and floured 23 cm/ 9 in cake tin (pan) and bake in a preheated oven at 180°C/350°F/gas mark 4 for 1 hour until a skewer inserted in the centre comes out clean.

Spiced Carrot Cake

Makes one 18 cm/7 in cake

175 g/6 oz/1 cup dates

120 ml/4 fl oz/½ cup water

175 g/6 oz/¾ cup butter or margarine, softened

2 eggs, lightly beaten

225 g/8 oz/2 cups self-raising (self-rising) flour

175 g/6 oz carrots, finely grated

25 g/1 oz/¼ cup ground almonds

Grated rind of 1 orange

2.5 ml/½ tsp ground mixed (apple-pie) spice

2.5 ml/½ tsp ground cinnamon

2.5 ml/½ tsp ground ginger

For the icing (frosting):

350 g/12 oz/1½ cups quark

25 g/1 oz/2 tbsp butter or margarine, softened

Grated rind of 1 orange

Place the dates and water in a small pan, bring to the boil, then simmer for 10 minutes until soft. Remove and discard the stones (pits), then chop the dates finely. Mix together the dates and the liquid, the butter or margarine and the eggs until creamy. Fold in all the remaining cake ingredients. Spoon the mixture into a greased and lined 18 cm/7 in cake tin (pan) and bake in a preheated oven at 180°C/350°F/gas mark 4 for 1 hour until a skewer inserted in the centre comes out clean. Leave to cool in the tin for 10 minutes before turning out on to a wire rack to finish cooling.

To make the icing, beat together all the ingredients until you have a spreadable consistency, adding a little more orange juice or water if necessary. Slice the cake in half horizontally, sandwich the layers together with half the icing and spread the remainder on top.

Carrot and Brown Sugar Cake

Makes one 18 cm/7 in cake

5 eggs, separated

200 g/7 oz/scant 1 cup soft brown sugar

15 ml/1 tbsp lemon juice

300 g/10 oz carrots, grated

225 g/8 oz/2 cups ground almonds

25 g/1 oz/¼ cup wholemeal (wholewheat) flour

5 ml/1 tsp ground cinnamon

25 g/1 oz/2 tbsp butter or margarine, melted

25 g/1 oz/2 tbsp caster (superfine) sugar

30 ml/2 tbsp single (light) cream

75 g/3 oz/¾ cup chopped mixed nuts

Beat the egg yolks until frothy, beat in the sugar until smooth, then beat in the lemon juice. Stir in one-third of the carrots, then one-third of the almonds and continue in this way until they are all combined. Stir in the flour and cinnamon. Whisk the egg whites until stiff, then fold them into the mixture using a metal spoon. Turn into a greased and lined deep 18 cm/7 in cake tin (pan) and bake in a preheated oven at 180°C/350°F/gas mark 4 for 1 hour. Cover the cake loosely with greaseproof (waxed) paper and reduce the oven temperature to 160°C/325°F/gas mark 3 for a further 15 minutes or until the cake shrinks slightly from the sides of the tin and the centre is still moist. Leave the cake in the tin until just warm, then turn out to finish cooling.

Combine the melted butter or margarine, sugar, cream and nuts, pour over the cake and cook under a medium grill (broiler) until golden brown.

Courgette and Marrow Cake

Makes one 20 cm/8 in cake

225 g/8 oz/1 cup caster (superfine) sugar

2 eggs, beaten

120 ml/4 fl oz/½ cup oil

100 g/4 oz/1 cup plain (all-purpose) flour

5 ml/1 tsp baking powder

2.5 ml/½ tsp bicarbonate of soda (baking soda)

2.5 ml/½ tsp salt

100 g/4 oz courgettes (zucchini), grated

100 g/4 oz crushed pineapple

50 g/2 oz/½ cup walnuts, chopped

5 ml/1 tsp vanilla essence (extract)

Beat together the sugar and eggs until pale and well blended. Beat in the oil and then the dry ingredients. Stir in the courgettes, pineapple, walnuts and vanilla essence. Spoon into a greased and floured 20 cm/8 in cake tin (pan) and bake in a preheated oven at 180°C/350°F/gas mark 4 for 1 hour until a skewer inserted in the centre comes out clean. Leave to cool in the tin for 30 minutes before turning out on to a wire rack to finish cooling.

Courgette and Orange Cake

Makes one 25 cm/10 in cake

225 g/8 oz/1 cup butter or margarine, softened

450 g/1 lb/2 cups soft brown sugar

4 eggs, lightly beaten

275 g/10 oz/2½ cups plain (all-purpose) flour

15 ml/1 tbsp baking powder

2.5 ml/½ tsp salt

5 ml/1 tsp ground cinnamon

2.5 ml/½ tsp grated nutmeg

A pinch of ground cloves

Grated rind and juice of 1 orange

225 g/8 oz/2 cups courgettes (zucchini), grated

Cream together the butter or margarine and sugar until light and fluffy. Gradually beat in the eggs, then fold in the flour, baking powder, salt and spices alternately with the orange rind and juice. Stir in the courgettes. Spoon into a greased and lined 25 cm/10 in cake tin (pan) and bake in a preheated oven at 180°C/350°F/gas mark 4 for 1 hour until golden brown and springy to the touch. If the top begins to over-brown towards the end of baking, cover with greaseproof (waxed) paper.

Spiced Courgette Cake

Makes one 25 cm/10 in cake

350 g/12 oz/3 cups plain (all-purpose) flour

10 ml/2 tsp baking powder

7.5 ml/1½ tsp ground cinnamon

5 ml/1 tsp bicarbonate of soda (baking soda)

2.5 ml/½ tsp salt

8 egg whites

450 g/1 lb/2 cups caster (superfine) sugar

100 g/4 oz/1 cup apple purée (sauce)

120 ml/4 fl oz/½ cup buttermilk

15 ml/1 tbsp vanilla essence (extract)

5 ml/1 tsp finely grated orange rind

350 g/12 oz/3 cups courgettes (zucchini), grated

75 g/3 oz/¾ cup walnuts, chopped

For the topping:

100 g/4 oz/½ cup cream cheese

25 g/1 oz/2 tbsp butter or margarine, softened

5 ml/1 tsp finely grated orange rind

10 ml/2 tsp orange juice

350 g/12 oz/2 cups icing (confectioners') sugar, sifted

Mix together the dry ingredients. Beat the egg whites until they form soft peaks. Slowly beat in the sugar, then the apple purée, buttermilk, vanilla essence and orange rind. Fold in the flour mixture, then the courgettes and walnuts. Spoon into a greased and floured 25 cm/10 in cake tin (pan) and bake in a preheated oven at 150°C/300°F/gas mark 2 for 1 hour until a skewer inserted in the centre comes out clean. Leave to cool in the tin.

Beat together all the topping ingredients until smooth, adding enough sugar to make a spreadable consistency. Spread over the cooled cake.

Pumpkin Cake

Makes one 23 x 33 cm/9 x 13 in cake

450 g/1 lb/2 cups caster (superfine) sugar

4 eggs, beaten

375 ml/13 fl oz/1½ cups oil

350 g/12 oz/3 cups plain (all-purpose) flour

15 ml/1 tbsp baking powder

10 ml/2 tsp bicarbonate of soda (baking soda)

10 ml/2 tsp ground cinnamon

2.5 ml/½ tsp ground ginger

A pinch of salt

225 g/8 oz diced cooked pumpkin

100 g/4 oz/1 cup walnuts, chopped

Beat together the sugar and eggs until well blended, then beat in the oil. Mix in the remaining ingredients. Spoon into a greased and floured 23 x 33 cm/ 9 x 13 in baking tin (pan) and bake in a preheated oven at 180°C/350°F/gas mark 4 for 1 hour until a skewer inserted in the centre comes out clean.

Fruited Pumpkin Cake

Makes one 20 cm/8 in cake

100 g/4 oz/½ cup butter or margarine, softened

150 g/5 oz/2/3 cup soft brown sugar

2 eggs, lightly beaten

225 g/8 oz cold cooked pumpkin

30 ml/2 tbsp golden (light corn) syrup

225 g/8 oz 1/1/3 cups dried mixed fruit (fruit cake mix)

225 g/8 oz/2 cups self-raising (self-rising) flour

50 g/2 oz/½ cup bran

Cream together the butter or margarine and sugar until light and fluffy. Gradually beat in the eggs, then fold in the remaining ingredients. Spoon into a greased and lined 20 cm/8 in cake tin (pan) and bake in a preheated oven at 160°C/325°F/gas mark 3 for 1¼ hours until a skewer inserted in the centre comes out clean.

Spiced Pumpkin Roll

Makes one 30 cm/12 in roll

75 g/3 oz/¾ cup plain (all-purpose) flour

5 ml/1 tsp bicarbonate of soda (baking soda)

5 ml/1 tsp ground ginger

2.5 ml/½ tsp grated nutmeg

10 ml/2 tsp ground cinnamon

A pinch of salt

1 egg

225 g/8 oz/1 cup caster (superfine) sugar

100 g/4 oz cooked pumpkin, diced

5 ml/1 tsp lemon juice

4 egg whites

50 g/2 oz/½ cup walnuts, chopped

50 g/2 oz/1/3 cup icing (confectioners') sugar, sifted

For the filling:

175 g/6 oz/1 cup icing (confectioners') sugar, sifted

100 g/4 oz/½ cup cream cheese

2.5 ml/½ tsp vanilla essence (extract)

Mix together the flour, bicarbonate of soda, spices and salt. Beat the egg until thick and pale, then beat in the sugar until the mixture is pale and creamy. Stir in the pumpkin and lemon juice. Fold in the flour mixture. In a clean bowl, beat the egg whites until stiff. Fold into the cake mix and spread in a greased and lined 30 x 12 cm/12 x 8 in Swiss roll tin (jelly roll pan) and sprinkle the walnuts over the top. Bake in a preheated oven at 190°C/375°F/gas mark 5 for 10 minutes until springy to the touch.

Sift the icing sugar over a clean tea towel (dish cloth) and turn the cake out on to the towel. Remove the lining paper and roll up the cake and towel, then leave to cool.

To make the filling, gradually beat the sugar into the cream cheese and vanilla essence until you have a spreadable mixture. Unroll the cake and spread the filling over the top. Roll up the cake again and chill before serving sprinkled with a little more icing sugar.

Rhubarb and Honey Cake

Makes two 450 g/1 lb cakes

250 g/9 oz/¾ cup clear honey

100 ml/4 fl oz/½ cup oil

1 egg

5 ml/1 tsp bicarbonate of soda (baking soda)

60 ml/4 tbsp water

350 g/12 oz/3 cups wholemeal (wholewheat) flour

10 ml/2 tsp salt

350 g/12 oz rhubarb, finely chopped

5 ml/1 tsp vanilla essence (extract)

50 g/2 oz/½ cup chopped mixed nuts (optional)

For the topping:

75 g/3 oz/1/3 cup muscovado sugar

5 ml/1 tsp ground cinnamon

15 g/½ oz/1 tbsp butter or margarine, softened

Mix together the honey and oil. Add the egg and beat well. Add the bicarbonate of soda to the water and leave to dissolve. Mix together the flour and salt. Add to the honey mixture alternately with the bicarbonate of soda mixture. Stir in the rhubarb, vanilla essence and nuts, if using. Pour into two greased 450 g/1 lb loaf tins (pans). Mix together the topping ingredients and spread over the cake mixture. Bake in a preheated oven at 180°C/350°F/gas mark 4 for 1 hour until springy to the touch.

Sweet Potato Cake

Makes one 23 cm/9 in cake

300 g/11 oz/2¾ cups plain (all-purpose) flour

15 ml/1 tbsp baking powder

5 ml/1 tsp ground cinnamon

5 ml/1 tsp grated nutmeg

A pinch of salt

350 g/12 oz/1¾ cups caster (superfine) sugar

375 ml/13 fl oz/1½ cups oil

60 ml/4 tbsp boiled water

4 eggs, separated

225 g/8 oz sweet potatoes, peeled and coarsely grated

100 g/4 oz/1 cup chopped mixed nuts

5 ml/1 tsp vanilla essence (extract)

For the icing (frosting):

225 g/8 oz/11/3 cups icing (confectioners') sugar, sifted

50 g/2 oz/¼ cup butter or margarine, softened

250 g/9 oz/1 medium tub cream cheese

50 g/2 oz/½ cup chopped mixed nuts

A pinch of ground cinnamon for sprinkling

Mix together the flour, baking powder, cinnamon, nutmeg and salt. Beat together the sugar and oil, then add the boiling water and beat until well blended. Add the egg yolks and flour mixture and mix until well blended. Stir in the sweet potatoes, nuts and vanilla essence. Beat the egg whites until stiff, then fold into the mixture. Spoon into two greased and floured 23 cm/9 in cake tins (pans) and bake in a preheated oven at 180°C/350°F/ gas mark 4 for 40 minutes until springy to the touch. Leave to cool in the tins for 5 minutes, then turn out on to a wire rack to finish cooling.

Mix together the icing sugar, butter or margarine and half the cream cheese. Spread half the remaining cream cheese over one cake, then spread the icing over the cheese. Sandwich the cakes together. Spread the remaining cream cheese over the top and sprinkle the nuts and cinnamon over the top before serving.

Italian Almond Cake

Makes one 20 cm/8 in cake

1 egg

150 ml/¼ pt/2/3 cup milk

2.5 ml/½ tsp almond essence (extract)

45 ml/3 tbsp butter, melted

350 g/12 oz/3 cups plain (all-purpose) flour

100 g/4 oz/½ cup caster (superfine) sugar

10 ml/2 tsp baking powder

2.5 ml/½ tsp salt

1 egg white

100 g/4 oz/1 cup almonds, chopped

Beat the egg in a bowl, then gradually add the milk, almond essence and melted butter, beating all the time. Add the flour, sugar, baking powder and salt and continue mixing until smooth. Spoon in to a greased and lined 20 cm/ 8 in cake tin (pan). Whisk the egg white until frothy, then brush generously over the top of the cake and sprinkle with the almonds. Bake in a preheated oven at 220°C/425°F/gas mark 7 for 25 minutes until golden brown and springy to the touch.

Almond and Coffee Torte

Makes one 23 cm/9 in cake

8 eggs, separated

175 g/6 oz/¾ cup caster (superfine) sugar

60 ml/4 tbsp strong black coffee

175 g/6 oz/1½ cups ground almonds

45 ml/3 tbsp semolina (cream of wheat)

100 g/4 oz/1 cup plain (all-purpose) flour

Beat the egg yolks and sugar until very thick and creamy. Add the coffee, ground almonds and semolina and beat well. Fold in the flour. Beat the egg whites until stiff, then fold into the mixture. Spoon into a greased 23 cm/9 in cake tin (pan) and bake in a preheated oven at 180°C/350°F/gas mark 4 for 45 minutes until springy to the touch.

Almond and Honey Cake

Makes one 20 cm/8 in cake

225 g/8 oz carrots, grated

75 g/3 oz/¾ cup almonds, chopped

2 eggs, beaten

100 ml/4 fl oz/½ cup clear honey

60 ml/4 tbsp oil

150 ml/¼ pt/2/3 cup milk

150 g/5 oz/1¼ cups wholemeal (wholewheat) flour

10 ml/2 tsp salt

10 ml/2 tsp bicarbonate of soda (baking soda)

15 ml/1 tbsp ground cinnamon

Mix together the carrots and nuts. Beat the eggs with the honey, oil and milk, then stir into the carrot mixture. Mix together the flour, salt, bicarbonate of soda and cinnamon and stir into the carrot mixture. Spoon the mixture into a greased and lined 20 cm/8 in square cake tin (pan) and bake in a preheated oven at 150°C/300°F/gas mark 2 for 1¾ hours until a skewer inserted in the centre comes out clean. Leave to cool in the tin for 10 minutes before turning out.

Almond and Lemon Cake

Makes one 23 cm/9 in cake

25 g/1 oz/¼ cup flaked (slivered) almonds

100 g/4 oz/½ cup butter or margarine, softened

100 g/4 oz/½ cup soft brown sugar

2 eggs, beaten

100 g/4 oz/1 cup self-raising (self-rising) flour

Grated rind of 1 lemon

For the syrup:

75 g/3 oz/1/3 cup caster (superfine) sugar

45–60 ml/3–4 tbsp lemon juice

Grease and line a 23 cm/9 in cake tin (pan) and sprinkle the almonds over the base. Cream together the butter and brown sugar. Beat in the eggs one at a time, then fold in the flour and lemon rind. Spoon into the prepared tin and level the surface. Bake in a preheated oven at 180°C/350°F/gas mark 4 for 20–25 minutes until well risen and springy to the touch.

Meanwhile, heat the caster sugar and lemon juice in a pan, stirring occasionally, until the sugar has dissolved. Remove the cake from the oven and leave to cool for 2 minutes, then turn out on to a wire rack with the base uppermost. Spoon over the syrup, then leave to cool completely.

Almond Cake with Orange

Makes one 20 cm/8 in cake

225 g/8 oz/1 cup butter or margarine, softened

225 g/8 oz/1 cup caster (superfine) sugar

4 eggs, separated

225 g/8 oz/2 cups plain (all-purpose) flour

10 ml/2 tsp baking powder

50 g/2 oz/½ cup ground almonds

5 ml/1 tsp grated orange rind

Cream together the butter or margarine and sugar until light and fluffy. Beat in the egg yolks, then fold in the flour, baking powder, ground almonds and orange rind. Whisk the egg whites until stiff, then fold into the mixture using a metal spoon. Spoon into a greased and lined 20 cm/8 in cake tin (pan) and bake in a preheated oven at 180°C/350°F/ gas mark 4 for 1 hour until a skewer inserted in the centre comes out clean.

Rich Almond Cake

Makes one 18 cm/7 in cake

100 g/4 oz/½ cup butter or margarine, softened

150 g/5 oz/2/3 cup caster (superfine) sugar

3 eggs, lightly beaten

75 g/3 oz/¾ cup ground almonds

50 g/2 oz/½ cup plain (all-purpose) flour

A few drops of almond essence (extract)

Cream together the butter or margarine and sugar until light and fluffy. Gradually beat in the eggs, then fold in the ground almonds, flour and almond essence. Spoon into a greased and lined 18 cm/7 in cake tin (pan) and bake in a preheated oven at 180°C/350°F/gas mark 4 for 45 minutes until springy to the touch.

Swedish Macaroon Cake

Makes one 23 cm/9 in cake

100 g/4 oz/1 cup ground almonds

75 g/3 oz/1/3 cup granulated sugar

5 ml/1 tsp baking powder

2 large egg whites, whisked

Mix together the almonds, sugar and baking powder. Stir in the egg whites until the mixture is thick and smooth. Spoon into a greased and lined 23 cm/9 in sandwich tin (pan) and bake in a preheated oven at 160°C/325°F/gas mark 3 for 20–25 minutes until risen and golden. Turn out very carefully from the tin as the cake is fragile.

Coconut Loaf

Makes one 450 g/1 lb loaf

100 g/4 oz/1 cup self-raising (self-rising) flour

225 g/8 oz/1 cup caster (superfine) sugar

100 g/4 oz/1 cup desiccated (shredded) coconut

1 egg

120 ml/4 fl oz/½ cup milk

A pinch of salt

Mix all the ingredients together well and spoon into a greased and lined 450 g/1 lb loaf tin (pan). Bake in a preheated oven at 180°C/350°F/gas mark 4 for about 1 hour until golden and springy to the touch.

Coconut Cake

Makes one 23 cm/9 in cake

75 g/3 oz/1/3 cup butter or margarine

150 ml/¼ pt/2/3 cup milk

2 eggs, lightly beaten

225 g/8 oz/1 cup caster (superfine) sugar

150 g/5 oz/1¼ cups self-raising (self-rising) flour

A pinch of salt

For the topping:

100 g/4 oz/½ cup butter or margarine

75 g/3 oz/¾ cup desiccated (shredded) coconut

60 ml/4 tbsp clear honey

45 ml/3 tbsp milk

50 g/2 oz/¼ cup soft brown sugar

Melt the butter or margarine in the milk, then leave to cool slightly. Beat together the eggs and caster sugar until light and frothy, then beat in the butter and milk mixture. Stir in the flour and salt to make a fairly thin mixture. Spoon into a greased and lined 23 cm/9 in cake tin (pan) and bake in a preheated oven at 180°C/350°F/gas mark 4 for 40 minutes until golden brown and springy to the touch.

Meanwhile, bring the topping ingredients to the boil in a pan. Turn out the warm cake and spoon over the topping mixture. Place under a hot grill (broiler) for a few minutes until the topping just begins to brown.

Golden Coconut Cake

Makes one 20 cm/8 in cake

100 g/4 oz/½ cup butter or margarine, softened

200 g/7 oz/scant 1 cup caster (superfine) sugar

200 g/7 oz/1¾ cups plain (all-purpose) flour

10 ml/2 tsp baking powder

A pinch of salt

175 ml/6 fl oz/¾ cup milk

3 egg whites

For the filling and topping:

150 g/5 oz/1¼ cups desiccated (shredded) coconut

200 g/7 oz/scant 1 cup caster (superfine) sugar

120 ml/4 fl oz/½ cup milk

120 ml/4 fl oz/½ cup water

3 egg yolks

Cream together the butter or margarine and sugar until light and fluffy. Stir the flour, baking powder and salt into the mixture alternately with the milk and water until you have a smooth batter. Beat the egg whites until stiff, then fold into the batter. Spoon the mixture into two greased 20 cm/8 in cake tins (pans) and bake in a preheated oven at 180°C/350°F/ gas mark 4 for 25 minutes until springy to the touch. Leave to cool.

Mix together the coconut, sugar, milk and egg yolks in a small pan. Heat over a gentle heat for a few minutes until the eggs are cooked, stirring continuously. Leave to cool. Sandwich the cakes together with half the coconut mixture, then spoon the rest on top.

Coconut Layer Cake

Makes one 9 x 18 cm/3½ x 7 in cake

100 g/4 oz/½ cup butter or margarine, softened

175 g/6 oz/¾ cup caster (superfine) sugar

3 eggs

175 g/6 oz/1½ cups plain (all-purpose) flour

5 ml/1 tsp baking powder

175 g/6 oz/1 cup sultanas (golden raisins)

120 ml/4 fl oz/½ cup milk

6 plain biscuits (cookies), crushed

100 g/4 oz/½ cup soft brown sugar

100 g/4 oz/1 cup desiccated (shredded) coconut

Cream together the butter or margarine and caster sugar until light and fluffy. Gradually beat in two of the eggs, then fold in the flour, baking powder and sultanas alternately with the milk. Spoon half the mixture into a greased and lined 450 g/1 lb loaf tin (pan). Mix together the remaining egg with the biscuit crumbs, brown sugar and coconut and sprinkle into the tin. Spoon in the remaining mixture and bake in a preheated oven at 180°C/350°F/gas mark 4 for 1 hour. Leave to cool in the tin for 30 minutes, then turn out on to a wire rack to finish cooling.

Coconut and Lemon Cake

Makes one 20 cm/8 in cake

100 g/4 oz/½ cup butter or margarine, softened

75 g/3 oz/1/3 cup soft brown sugar

Grated rind of 1 lemon

1 egg, beaten

A few drops of almond essence (extract)

350 g/12 oz/3 cups self-raising (self-rising) flour

60 ml/4 tbsp raspberry jam (conserve)

For the topping:

1 egg, beaten

75 g/3 oz/1/3 cup soft brown sugar

225 g/8 oz/2 cups desiccated (shredded) coconut

Cream together the butter or margarine, sugar and lemon rind until light and fluffy. Gradually beat in the egg and almond essence, then fold in the flour. Spoon the mixture into a greased and lined 20 cm/8 in cake tin (pan). Spoon the jam over the mixture. Beat together the topping ingredients and spread over the mixture. Bake in a preheated oven at 180°C/350°F/gas mark 4 for 30 minutes until springy to the touch. Leave to cool in the tin.

Coconut New Year Cake

Makes one 18 cm/7 in cake

100 g/4 oz/½ cup butter or margarine, softened

100 g/4 oz/½ cup caster (superfine) sugar

2 eggs, lightly beaten

75 g/3 oz/¾ cup plain (all-purpose) flour

45 ml/3 tbsp desiccated (shredded) coconut

30 ml/2 tbsp rum

A few drops of almond essence (extract)

A few drops of lemon essence (extract)

Cream together the butter and sugar until light and fluffy. Gradually beat in the eggs, then fold in the flour and coconut. Stir in the rum and essences. Spoon into a greased and lined 18 cm/7 in cake tin (pan) and level the surface. Bake in a preheated oven at 190°C/375°F/ gas mark 5 for 45 minutes until a skewer inserted in the centre comes out clean. Leave to cool in the tin.

Coconut and Sultana Cake

Makes one 23 cm/9 in cake

100 g/4 oz/½ cup butter or margarine, softened

175 g/6 oz/¾ cup caster (superfine) sugar

2 eggs, lightly beaten

175 g/6 oz/1½ cups plain (all-purpose) flour

5 ml/1 tsp baking powder

A pinch of salt

175 g/6 oz/1 cup sultanas (golden raisins)

120 ml/4 fl oz/½ cup milk

For the filling:

1 egg, lightly beaten

50 g/2 oz/½ cup plain biscuit (cookie) crumbs

100 g/4 oz/½ cup soft brown sugar

100 g/4 oz/1 cup desiccated (shredded) coconut

Cream together the butter or margarine and caster sugar until light and fluffy. Gradually mix in the eggs. Fold in the flour, baking powder, salt and sultanas with enough of the milk to make a soft dropping consistency. Spoon half the mixture into a greased 23 cm/9 in cake tin (pan). Mix together the filling ingredients and spoon over the mixture, then top with the remaining cake mix. Bake in a preheated oven at 180°C/350°F/gas mark 4 for 1 hour until springy to the touch and beginning to shrink away from the sides of the tin. Leave to cool in the tin before turning out.

Crunchy-topped Nut Cake

Makes one 23 cm/9 in cake

225 g/8 oz/1 cup butter or margarine, softened

225 g/8 oz/1 cup caster (superfine) sugar

2 eggs, lightly beaten

225 g/8 oz/2 cups plain (all-purpose) flour

2.5 ml/½ tsp bicarbonate of soda (baking soda)

2.5 ml/½ tsp cream of tartar

200 ml/7 fl oz/scant 1 cup milk

For the topping:
100 g/4 oz/1 cup chopped mixed nuts

100 g/4 oz/½ cup soft brown sugar

5 ml/1 tsp ground cinnamon

Cream together the butter or margarine and caster sugar until light and fluffy. Gradually beat in the eggs, then fold in the flour, bicarbonate of soda and cream of tartar alternately with the milk. Spoon into a greased and lined 23 cm/9 in cake tin (pan). Mix together the nuts, brown sugar and cinnamon and sprinkle over the top of the cake. Bake in a preheated oven at 180°C/350°F/gas mark 4 for 40 minutes until golden brown and shrinking away from the sides of the tin. Leave to cool in the tin for 10 minutes, then turn out on to a wire rack to finish cooling.

Mixed Nut Cake

Makes one 23 cm/9 in cake

100 g/4 oz/½ cup butter or margarine, softened

225 g/8 oz/1 cup caster (superfine) sugar

1 egg, beaten

225 g/8 oz/2 cups self-raising (self-rising) flour

10 ml/2 tsp baking powder

A pinch of salt

250 ml/8 fl oz/1 cup milk

5 ml/1 tsp vanilla essence (extract)

2.5 ml/½ tsp lemon essence (extract)

100 g/4 oz/1 cup chopped mixed nuts

Cream together the butter or margarine and sugar until light and fluffy. Gradually beat in the egg. Mix together the flour, baking powder and salt and add to the mixture alternately with the milk and essences. Fold in the nuts. Spoon into two greased and lined 23 cm/9 in cake tins (pans) and bake in a preheated oven at 180°F/350°F/gas mark 4 for 40 minutes until a skewer inserted in the centre comes out clean.

Greek Nut Cake

Makes one 25 cm/10 in cake

100 g/4 oz/½ cup butter or margarine, softened

225 g/8 oz/1 cup caster (superfine) sugar

3 eggs, lightly beaten

250 g/9 oz/2¼ cups plain (all-purpose) flour

225 g/8 oz/2 cups walnuts, ground

10 ml/2 tsp baking powder

5 ml/1 tsp ground cinnamon

1.5 ml/¼ tsp ground cloves

A pinch of salt

75 ml/5 tbsp milk

For the honey syrup:

175 g/6 oz/¾ cup caster (superfine) sugar

75 g/3 oz/¼ cup clear honey

15 ml/1 tbsp lemon juice

250 ml/8 fl oz/1 cup boiling water

Cream together the butter or margarine and sugar until light and fluffy. Gradually beat in the eggs, then fold in the flour, walnuts, baking powder, spices and salt. Add the milk and mix until smooth. Spoon into a greased and floured 25 cm/10 in cake tin (pan) and bake in a preheated oven at 180°C/350°F/ gas mark 4 for 40 minutes until springy to the touch. Leave to cool in the tin for 10 minutes, then transfer to a wire rack.

To make the syrup, mix together the sugar, honey, lemon juice and water and heat until dissolved. Prick the warm cake all over with a fork, then spoon over the honey syrup.

Iced Walnut Cake

Makes one 18 cm/7 in cake

100 g/4 oz/½ cup butter or margarine, softened

100 g/4 oz/½ cup caster (superfine) sugar

2 eggs, lightly beaten

100 g/4 oz/1 cup self-raising (self-rising) flour

100 g/4 oz/1 cup walnuts, chopped

A pinch of salt

For the icing (frosting):

450 g/1 lb/2 cups granulated sugar

150 ml/¼ pt/2/3 cup water

2 egg whites

A few walnut halves to decorate

Cream together the butter or margarine and caster sugar until light and fluffy. Gradually beat in the eggs, then fold in the flour, nuts and salt. Spoon the mixture into two greased and lined 18 cm/7 in cake tins (pans) and bake in a preheated oven at 180°C/350°F/gas mark 4 for 25 minutes until well risen and springy to the touch. Leave to cool.

Dissolve the granulated sugar in the water over a low heat, stirring continuously, then bring to the boil and continue to boil, without stirring, until a drop of the mixture forms a soft ball when dropped into cold water. Meanwhile, whisk the egg whites in a clean bowl until stiff. Pour the syrup on to the egg white and whisk until the mixture is thick enough to coat the back of a spoon. Sandwich the cakes together with a layer of the icing, then spread the rest over the top and sides of the cake and decorate with walnut halves.

Walnut Cake with Chocolate Cream

Makes one 18 cm/7 in cake

3 eggs

75 g/3 oz/1/3 cup soft brown sugar

50 g/2 oz/½ cup wholemeal (wholewheat) flour

25 g/1 oz/¼ cup cocoa (unsweetened chocolate) powder

For the icing (frosting):

150 g/5 oz/1¼ cups plain (semi-sweet) chocolate

225 g/8 oz/1 cup low-fat cream cheese

45 ml/3 tbsp icing (confectioners') sugar, sifted

75 g/3 oz/¾ cup walnuts, chopped

15 ml/1 tbsp brandy (optional)

Grated chocolate to garnish

Whisk together the eggs and brown sugar until pale and thick. Fold in the flour and cocoa. Spoon the mixture into two greased and lined 18 cm/7 in sandwich tins (pans) and bake in a preheated oven at 190°C/375°F/gas mark 5 for 15–20 minutes until well risen and springy to the touch. Remove from the tins and leave to cool.

Melt the chocolate in a heatproof bowl set over a pan of gently simmering water. Remove from the heat and stir in the cream cheese and icing sugar, then stir in the nuts and brandy, if using. Sandwich the cakes together with most of the filling and spread the remainder on top. Garnish with the grated chocolate.

Walnut Cake with Honey and Cinnamon

Makes one 23 cm/9 in cake

225 g/8 oz/2 cups plain (all-purpose) flour

10 ml/2 tsp baking powder

5 ml/1 tsp bicarbonate of soda (baking soda)

5 ml/1 tsp ground cinnamon

A pinch of salt

100 g/4 oz/1 cup plain yoghurt

75 ml/5 tbsp oil

100 g/4 oz/1/3 cup clear honey

1 egg, lightly beaten

5 ml/1 tsp vanilla essence (extract)

For the filling:

50 g/2 oz/½ cup chopped walnuts

225 g/8 oz/1 cup soft brown sugar

10 ml/2 tsp ground cinnamon

30 ml/2 tbsp oil

Mix together the dry ingredients for the cake and make a well in the centre. Whisk together the remaining cake ingredients and blend into the dry ingredients. Mix together the ingredients for the filling. Spoon half the cake mixture into a greased and floured 23 cm/9 in cake tin (pan) and sprinkle with half the filling. Add the remaining cake mixture, then the remaining filling. Bake in a preheated oven at 180°C/350°F/ gas mark 4 for 30 minutes until well risen and golden brown and beginning to shrink away from the sides of the pan.

Almond and Honey Bars

Makes 10

15 g/½ oz fresh yeast or 20 ml/4 tsp dried yeast

45 ml/3 tbsp caster (superfine) sugar

120 ml/4 fl oz/½ cup warm milk

300 g/11 oz/2¾ cups plain (all-purpose) flour

A pinch of salt

1 egg, lightly beaten

50 g/2 oz/¼ cup butter or margarine, softened

300 ml/½ pt/1¼ cups double (heavy) cream

30 ml/2 tbsp icing (confectioners') sugar, sifted

45 ml/3 tbsp clear honey

300 g/11 oz/2¾ cups flaked (slivered) almonds

Mix the yeast, 5 ml/1 tsp of the caster sugar and a little of the milk and leave in a warm place for 20 minutes until frothy. Mix the remaining sugar with the flour and salt and make a well in the centre. Gradually blend in the egg, butter or margarine, yeast mixture and remaining warm milk and mix to a soft dough. Knead on a lightly floured surface until smooth and elastic. Place in an oiled bowl, cover with oiled clingfilm (plastic wrap) and leave in a warm place for 45 minutes until doubled in size.

Knead the dough again, then roll out and place in a 30 x 20 cm/12 x 8 in greased cake tin (pan), prick all over with a fork, cover and leave in a warm place for 10 minutes.

Put 120 ml/4 fl oz/½ cup of the cream, the icing sugar and honey in a small pan and bring to the boil. Remove from the heat and mix in the almonds. Spread over the dough, then bake in a preheated oven at 200°C/400°F/gas mark 6 for 20 minutes until golden and springy to the touch, covering with greaseproof (waxed) paper if the top begins to brown too much before the end of cooking. Turn out and leave to cool.

Cut the cake in half horizontally. Whip the remaining cream until stiff and spread over the bottom half of the cake. Top with the almond-covered half of the cake and cut into bars.

Apple and Blackcurrant Crumble Bars

Makes 12

175 g/6 oz/1½ cups plain (all-purpose) flour

5 ml/1 tsp baking powder

A pinch of salt

175 g/6 oz/¾ cup butter or margarine

225 g/8 oz/1 cup soft brown sugar

100 g/4 oz/1 cup rolled oats

450 g/1 lb cooking (tart) apples, peeled, cored and sliced

30 ml/2 tbsp cornflour (cornstarch)

10 ml/2 tsp ground cinnamon

2.5 ml/½ tsp grated nutmeg

2.5 ml/½ tsp ground allspice

225 g/8 oz blackcurrants

Mix the flour, baking powder and salt, then rub in the butter or margarine. Stir in the sugar and oats. Spoon half into the base of a greased and lined 25 cm/9 in square cake tin (pan). Mix the apples, cornflour and spices and spread over. Top with the blackcurrants. Spoon over the remaining mixture and level the top. Bake in a preheated oven at 180°C/350°F/gas mark 4 for 30 minutes until springy. Leave to cool, then cut into bars.

Apricot and Oatmeal Bars

Makes 24

75 g/3 oz/½ cup dried apricots

25 g/1 oz/3 tbsp sultanas (golden raisins)

250 ml/8 fl oz/1 cup water

5 ml/1 tsp lemon juice

150 g/5 oz/2/3 cup soft brown sugar

50 g/2 oz/½ cup desiccated (shredded) coconut

50 g/2 oz/½ cup plain (all-purpose) flour

2.5 ml/½ tsp bicarbonate of soda (baking soda)

100 g/4 oz/1 cup rolled oats

50 g/2 oz/¼ cup butter, melted

Place the apricots, sultanas, water, lemon juice and 30 ml/2 tbsp of the brown sugar in a small pan and stir over a low heat until thick. Stir in the coconut and leave to cool. Mix the flour, bicarbonate of soda, oats and the remaining sugar, then blend in the melted butter. Press half the oat mixture into the base of a greased 20 cm/8 in square baking tin (pan), then spread the apricot mixture on top. Cover with the remaining oat mixture and press down lightly. Bake in a preheated oven at 180°C/ 350°F/gas mark 4 for 30 minutes until golden. Leave to cool, then cut into bars.

Apricot Crunchies

Makes 16

100 g/4 oz/2/3 cup ready-to-eat dried apricots

120 ml/4 fl oz/½ cup orange juice

100 g/4 oz/½ cup butter or margarine

75 g/3 oz/¾ cup wholemeal (wholewheat) flour

75 g/3 oz/¾ cup rolled oats

75 g/3 oz/1/3 cup demerara sugar

Soak the apricots in the orange juice for at least 30 minutes until soft, then drain and chop. Rub the butter or margarine into the flour until the mixture resembles breadcrumbs. Stir in the oats and sugar. Press half the mixture into a greased 30 x 20 cm/12 x 8 in Swiss roll tin (jelly roll pan) and sprinkle with the apricots. Spread the remaining mixture on top and press down gently. Bake in a preheated oven at 180°C/350°F/gas mark 4 for 25 minutes until golden brown. Leave to cool in the tin before turning out and cutting into bars.

Nutty Banana Bars

Makes about 14

50 g/2 oz/¼ cup butter or margarine, softened

75 g/3 oz/1/3 cup caster (superfine) or soft brown sugar

2 large bananas, chopped

175 g/6 oz/1½ cups plain (all-purpose) flour

7.5 ml/1½ tsp baking powder

2 eggs, beaten

50 g/2 oz/½ cup walnuts, roughly chopped

Cream together the butter or margarine and sugar. Mash the bananas and stir into the mixture. Mix the flour and baking powder. Add the flour, eggs and nuts to the bananas mixture and beat well. Spoon into a greased and lined 18 x 28 cm/7 x 11 in cake tin, level the surface and bake in a preheated oven at 160°C/325°F/gas mark 3 for 30–35 minutes until springy to the touch. Leave to cool for a few minutes in the tin, then turn out on to a wire rack to finish cooling. Cut into about 14 bars.

American Brownies

Makes about 15

2 large eggs

225 g/8 oz/1 cup caster (superfine) sugar

50 g/2 oz/¼ cup butter or margarine, melted

2.5 ml/½ tsp vanilla essence (extract)

75 g/3 oz/¾ cup plain (all-purpose) flour

45 ml/3 tbsp cocoa (unsweetened chocolate) powder

2.5 ml/½ tsp baking powder

A pinch of salt

50 g/2 oz/½ cup walnuts, roughly chopped

Whisk together the eggs and sugar until thick and creamy. Beat in the butter and vanilla essence. Sift in the flour, cocoa, baking powder and salt and fold into the mixture with the walnuts. Turn into a well greased 20 cm/8 in square cake tin (pan). Bake in a preheated oven at 180°C/350°F/gas mark 4 for 40–45 minutes until springy to the touch. Leave in the tin for 10 minutes, then cut into squares and transfer to a wire rack while still warm.

Chocolate Fudge Brownies

Makes about 16

225 g/8 oz/1 cup butter or margarine

175 g/6 oz/¾ cup granulated sugar

350 g/12 oz/3 cups self-raising (self-rising) flour

30 ml/2 tbsp cocoa (unsweetened chocolate) powder

For the icing (frosting):
175 g/6 oz/1 cup icing (confectioners') sugar, sifted

30 ml/2 tbsp cocoa (unsweetened chocolate) powder

Boiling water

Melt the butter or margarine, then stir in the granulated sugar. Stir in the flour and cocoa. Press into a lined 18 x 28 cm/7 x 11 in baking tin (pan). Bake in a preheated oven at 180°C/ 350°F/gas mark 4 for about 20 minutes until springy to the touch.

To make the icing, sift the icing sugar and cocoa into a bowl and add a drop of boiling water. Stir until well blended, adding a drop or so more water if necessary. Ice the brownies while still warm (but not hot), then leave to cool before cutting into squares.

Walnut and Chocolate Brownies

Makes 12

50 g/2 oz/½ cup plain (semi-sweet) chocolate

75 g/3 oz/1/3 cup butter or margarine

225 g/8 oz/1 cup caster (superfine) sugar

75 g/3 oz/¾ cup plain (all-purpose) flour

75 g/3 oz/¾ cup walnuts, chopped

50 g/2 oz/½ cup chocolate chips

2 eggs, beaten

2.5 ml/½ tsp vanilla essence (extract)

Melt the chocolate and butter or margarine in a heatproof bowl set over a pan of gently simmering water. Remove from the heat and stir in the remaining ingredients. Spoon into a greased and lined 20 cm/8 in cake tin (pan) and bake in a preheated oven at 180°C/350°F/gas mark 4 for 30 minutes until a skewer inserted in the centre comes out clean. Leave to cool in the tin, then cut into squares.

Butter Bars

Makes 16

100 g/4 oz/½ cup butter or margarine, softened

100 g/4 oz/½ cup caster (superfine) sugar

1 egg, separated

100 g/4 oz/1 cup plain (all-purpose) flour

25 g/1 oz/¼ cup chopped mixed nuts

Cream together the butter or margarine and sugar until light and fluffy. Blend in the egg yolk, then stir in the flour and nuts to make a fairly stiff mixture. If it is too stiff, add a little milk; if it is runny, stir in a little more flour. Spoon the dough into a greased 30 x 20 cm/12 x 8 in Swiss roll tin (jelly roll pan). Beat the egg white until frothy and spread over the mixture. Bake in a preheated oven at 180°C/ 350°F/gas mark 4 for 30 minutes until golden. Leave to cool, then cut into bars.

Cherry Toffee Traybake

Makes 12

100 g/4 oz/1 cup almonds

225 g/8 oz/1 cup glacé (candied) cherries, halved

225 g/8 oz/1 cup butter or margarine, softened

225 g/8 oz/1 cup caster (superfine) sugar

3 eggs, beaten

100 g/4 oz/1 cup self-raising (self-rising) flour

50 g/2 oz/½ cup ground almonds

5 ml/1 tsp baking powder

5 ml/1 tsp almond essence (extract)

Sprinkle the almonds and cherries over the base of a greased and lined 20 cm/ 8 in cake tin (pan). Melt 50 g/2 oz/¼ cup of the butter or margarine with 50 g/2 oz/ ¼ cup of the sugar, then pour it over the cherries and nuts. Beat the remaining butter or margarine and sugar until light and fluffy, then beat in the eggs and mix in the flour, ground almonds, baking powder and almond essence. Spoon the mixture into the tin and level the top. Bake in a preheated oven at 160°C/325°F/gas mark 3 for 1 hour. Leave to cool in the tin for a few minutes, then invert carefully on to a wire rack, scraping any of the topping off the lining paper if necessary. Leave to cool completely before cutting.

Chocolate Chip Traybake

Makes 24

100 g/4 oz/½ cup butter or margarine, softened

100 g/4 oz/½ cup soft brown sugar

50 g/2 oz/¼ cup caster (superfine) sugar

1 egg

5 ml/1 tsp vanilla essence (extract)

100 g/4 oz/1 cup plain (all-purpose) flour

2.5 ml/½ tsp bicarbonate of soda (baking soda)

A pinch of salt

100 g/4 oz/1 cup chocolate chips

Cream together the butter or margarine and sugars until light and fluffy, then gradually add the egg and vanilla essence. Stir in the flour, bicarbonate of soda and salt. Stir in the chocolate chips. Spoon into a greased and floured 25 cm/12 in square baking tin (pan) and bake in a pre-heated oven at 190°C/375°F/gas mark 2 for 15 minutes until golden brown. Leave to cool, then cut into squares.

Cinnamon Crumble Layer

Makes 12

For the base:

100 g/4 oz/½ cup butter or margarine, softened

30 ml/2 tbsp clear honey

2 eggs, lightly beaten

100 g/4 oz/1 cup plain (all-purpose) flour

For the crumble:

75 g/3 oz/1/3 cup butter or margarine

75 g/3 oz/¾ cup plain (all-purpose) flour

75 g/3 oz/¾ cup rolled oats

5 ml/1 tsp ground cinnamon

50 g/2 oz/¼ cup demerara sugar

Cream together the butter or margarine and honey until light and fluffy. Gradually beat in the eggs, then fold in the flour. Spoon half the mixture into a greased 20 cm/8 in square cake tin (pan) and level the surface.

To make the crumble, rub the butter or margarine into the flour until the mixture resembles breadcrumbs. Stir in the oats, cinnamon and sugar. Spoon half the crumble into the tin, then top with the remaining cake mix, then the remaining crumble. Bake in a preheated oven at 190°C/375°F/gas mark 5 for about 35 minutes until a skewer inserted in the centre comes out clean. Leave to cool, then cut into bars.

Gooey Cinnamon Bars

Makes 16

225 g/8 oz/2 cups plain (all-purpose) flour

10 ml/2 tsp baking powder

225 g/8 oz/1 cup soft brown sugar

15 ml/1 tbsp melted butter

250 ml/8 fl oz/1 cup milk

30 ml/2 tbsp demerara sugar

10 ml/2 tsp ground cinnamon

25 g/1 oz/2 tbsp butter, chilled and diced

Mix together the flour, baking powder and sugar. Stir in the melted butter and milk and blend together well. Press the mixture into two 23 cm/9 in square cake tins (pans). Sprinkle the tops with the demerara sugar and cinnamon, then press pieces of butter over the surface. Bake in a preheated oven at 180°C/350°F/ gas mark 4 for 30 minutes. The butter will make holes in the mixture and go gooey as it cooks.

Coconut Bars

Makes 16

75 g/3 oz/1/3 cup butter or margarine

100 g/4 oz/1 cup plain (all-purpose) flour

30 ml/2 tbsp caster (superfine) sugar

2 eggs

100 g/4 oz/½ cup soft brown sugar

A pinch of salt

175 g/6 oz/1½ cups desiccated (shredded) coconut

50 g/2 oz/½ cup chopped mixed nuts

Orange Icing

Rub the butter or margarine into the flour until the mixture resembles breadcrumbs. Stir in the sugar and press into an ungreased 23 cm/9 in square baking tin (pan). Bake in a preheated oven at 190°C/350°F/gas mark 4 for 15 minutes until just set.

Blend together the eggs, brown sugar and salt, then stir in the coconut and nuts and spread over the base. Bake for 20 minutes until set and golden. Ice with orange icing when cool. Cut into bars.

Coconut and Jam Sandwich Bars

Makes 16

25 g/1 oz/2 tbsp butter or margarine

175 g/6 oz/1½ cups self-raising (self-rising) flour

225 g/8 oz/1 cup caster (superfine) sugar

2 egg yolks

75 ml/5 tbsp water

175 g/6 oz/1½ cups desiccated (shredded) coconut

4 egg whites

50 g/2 oz/½ cup plain (all-purpose) flour

100 g/4 oz/1/3 cup strawberry jam (conserve)

Rub the butter or margarine into the self-raising flour, then stir in 50 g/ 2 oz/¼ cup of the sugar. Beat together the egg yolks and 45 ml/3 tbsp of the water and stir into the mixture. Press into the base of a greased 30 x 20 cm/12 x 8 in Swiss roll tin (jelly roll pan) and prick with a fork. Bake in a preheated oven at 180°C/350°F/gas mark 4 for 12 minutes. Leave to cool.

Place the coconut, the remaining sugar and water and one egg white in a pan and stir over a low heat until the mixture becomes lumpy without letting it brown. Leave to cool. Mix in the plain flour. Whisk the remaining egg whites until stiff, then fold into the mixture. Spread the jam over the base, then spread with the coconut topping. Bake in the oven for 30 minutes until golden brown. Leave to cool in the tin before cutting into bars.

Date and Apple Traybake

Makes 12

1 cooking (tart) apple, peeled, cored and chopped

225 g/8 oz/1 1/3 cups stoned (pitted) dates, chopped

150 ml/¼ pt/2/3 cup water

350 g/12 oz/3 cups rolled oats

175 g/6 oz/¾ cup butter or margarine, melted

45 ml/3 tbsp demerara sugar

5 ml/1 tsp ground cinnamon

Place the apples, dates and water in a pan and simmer gently for about 5 minutes until the apples are soft. Leave to cool. Mix together the oats, butter or margarine, sugar and cinnamon. Spoon half into a greased 20 cm/8 in square cake tin (pan) and level the surface. Top with the apple and date mixture, then cover with the remaining oat mixture and level the surface. Press down gently. Bake in a preheated oven at 190°C/375°F/gas mark 5 for about 30 minutes until golden brown. Leave to cool, then cut into bars.

Date Slices

Makes 12

225 g/8 oz/1 1/3 cups stoned (pitted) dates, chopped

30 ml/2 tbsp clear honey

30 ml/2 tbsp lemon juice

225 g/8 oz/1 cup butter or margarine

225 g/8 oz/2 cups wholemeal (wholewheat) flour

225 g/8 oz/2 cups rolled oats

75 g/3 oz/1/3 cup soft brown sugar

Simmer the dates, honey and lemon juice over a low heat for a few minutes until the dates are soft. Rub the butter or margarine into the flour and oats until the mixture resembles breadcrumbs, then stir in the sugar. Spoon half the mixture into a greased and lined 20 cm/8 in square cake tin (pan). Spoon the date mixture over the top, then finish with the remaining cake mixture. Press down firmly. Bake in a preheated oven at 190°C/375°F/gas mark 5 for 35 minutes until springy to the touch. Leave to cool in the tin, cutting into slices while still warm.

Grandma's Date Bars

Makes 16

100 g/4 oz/½ cup butter or margarine, softened

225 g/8 oz/1 cup soft brown sugar

2 eggs, lightly beaten

175 g/6 oz/1½ cups plain (all-purpose) flour

2.5 ml/½ tsp bicarbonate of soda (baking soda)

5 ml/1 tsp ground cinnamon

A pinch of ground cloves

A pinch of grated nutmeg

175 g/6 oz/1 cup stoned (pitted) dates, chopped

Cream together the butter or margarine and sugar until light and fluffy. Gradually add the eggs, beating well after each addition. Stir in the remaining ingredients until well blended. Spoon into a greased and floured 23 cm/9 in square baking tin (pan) and bake in a preheated oven at 180°C/350°F/gas mark 4 for 25 minutes until a skewer inserted in the centre comes out clean. Leave to cool, then cut into bars.

Date and Oatmeal Bars

Makes 16

175 g/6 oz/1 cup stoned (pitted) dates, chopped

15 ml/1 tbsp clear honey

30 ml/2 tbsp water

225 g/8 oz/2 cups wholemeal (wholewheat) flour

100 g/4 oz/1 cup rolled oats

100 g/4 oz/½ cup soft brown sugar

150 g/5 oz/2/3 cup butter or margarine, melted

Simmer the dates, honey and water in a small pan until the dates are soft. Mix together the flour, oats and sugar, then blend in the melted butter or margarine. Press half the mixture into a greased 18 cm/7 in square cake tin (pan), sprinkle with the date mixture, then top with the remaining oat mixture and press down gently. Bake in a preheated oven at 180°C/350°F/gas mark 4 for 1 hour until firm and golden. Leave to cool in the tin, cutting into bars while still warm.

Date and Walnut Bars

Makes 12

100 g/4 oz/½ cup butter or margarine, softened

150 g/5 oz/2/3 cup caster (superfine) sugar

1 egg, lightly beaten

100 g/4 oz/1 cup self-raising (self-rising) flour

225 g/8 oz/11/3 cups stoned (pitted) dates, chopped

100 g/4 oz/1 cup walnuts, chopped

15 ml/1 tbsp milk (optional)

100 g/4 oz/1 cup plain (semi-sweet) chocolate

Cream together the butter or margarine and sugar until light and fluffy. Mix in the egg, then the flour, dates and walnuts, adding a little of the milk if the mixture is too stiff. Spoon into a greased 30 x 20 cm/12 x 8 in Swiss roll tin (jelly roll pan) and bake in a preheated oven at 180°C/350°F/gas mark 4 for 30 minutes until springy to the touch. Leave to cool.

Melt the chocolate in a heatproof bowl set over a pan of gently simmering water. Spread over the mixture and leave to cool and set. Cut into bars with a sharp knife.

Fig Bars

Makes 16

225 g/8 oz fresh figs, chopped

30 ml/2 tbsp clear honey

15 ml/1 tbsp lemon juice

225 g/8 oz/2 cups wholemeal (wholewheat) flour

225 g/8 oz/2 cups rolled oats

225 g/8 oz/1 cup butter or margarine

75 g/3 oz/1/3 cup soft brown sugar

Simmer the figs, honey and lemon juice over a low heat for 5 minutes. Allow to cool slightly. Mix together the flour and oats, then rub in the butter or margarine and stir in the sugar. Press half the mixture into a greased 20 cm/8 in square cake tin (pan), then spoon the fig mixture over the top. Cover with the remaining cake mixture and press down firmly. Bake in a preheated oven at 180°C/350°F/gas mark 4 for 30 minutes until golden brown. Leave in the tin to cool, then cut into slices while still warm.

Flapjacks

Makes 16

75 g/3 oz/1/3 cup butter or margarine

50 g/2 oz/3 tbsp golden (light corn) syrup

100 g/4 oz/½ cup soft brown sugar

175 g/6 oz/1½ cups rolled oats

Melt the butter or margarine with the syrup and sugar, then stir in the oats. Press into a greased 20 cm/8 in square tin and bake in a preheated oven at 180°C/350°F/gas mark 4 for about 20 minutes until lightly golden. Leave to cool slightly before cutting into bars, then leave in the tin to cool completely before turning out.

Cherry Flapjacks

Makes 16

75 g/3 oz/1/3 cup butter or margarine

50 g/2 oz/3 tbsp golden (light corn) syrup

100 g/4 oz/½ cup soft brown sugar

175 g/6 oz/1½ cups rolled oats

100 g/4 oz/1 cup glacé (candied) cherries, chopped

Melt the butter or margarine with the syrup and sugar, then stir in the oats and cherries. Press into a greased 20 cm/ 8 in square cake tin (pan) and bake in a preheated oven at 180°C/350°F/gas mark 4 for about 20 minutes until lightly golden. Leave to cool slightly before cutting into bars, then leave in the tin to cool completely before turning out.

Chocolate Flapjacks

Makes 16

75 g/3 oz/1/3 cup butter or margarine

50 g/2 oz/3 tbsp golden (light corn) syrup

100 g/4 oz/½ cup soft brown sugar

175 g/6 oz/1½ cups rolled oats

100 g/4 oz/1 cup chocolate chips

Melt the butter or margarine with the syrup and sugar, then stir in the oats and chocolate chips. Press into a greased 20 cm/8 in square cake tin (pan) and bake in a preheated oven at 180°C/350°F/gas mark 4 for about 20 minutes until lightly golden. Leave to cool slightly before cutting into bars, then leave in the tin to cool completely before turning out.

Fruit Flapjacks

Makes 16

75 g/3 oz/1/3 cup butter or margarine

100 g/4 oz/½ cup soft brown sugar

50 g/2 oz/3 tbsp golden (light corn) syrup

175 g/6 oz/1½ cups rolled oats

75 g/3 oz/½ cup raisins, sultanas or other dried fruit

Melt the butter or margarine with the sugar and syrup, then stir in the oats and raisins. Press into a greased 20 cm/ 8 in square cake tin (pan) and bake in a preheated oven at 180°C/350°F/gas mark 4 for about 20 minutes until lightly golden. Leave to cool slightly before cutting into bars, then leave in the tin to cool completely before turning out.

Fruit and Nut Flapjacks

Makes 16

75 g/3 oz/1/3 cup butter or margarine

100 g/4 oz/1/3 cup clear honey

50 g/2 oz/1/3 cup raisins

50 g/2 oz/½ cup walnuts, chopped

175 g/6 oz/1½ cups rolled oats

Melt the butter or margarine with the honey over a low heat. Stir in the raisins, walnuts and oats and mix together well. Spoon into a greased 23 cm/9 in square cake tin (pan) and bake in a preheated oven at 180°C/350°F/gas mark 4 for 25 minutes. Leave to cool in the tin, cutting into bars while still warm.

Ginger Flapjacks

Makes 16

75 g/3 oz/1/3 cup butter or margarine

100 g/4 oz/½ cup soft brown sugar

50 g/2 oz/3 tbsp syrup from a jar of stem ginger

175 g/6 oz/1½ cups rolled oats

4 pieces stem ginger, finely chopped

Melt the butter or margarine with the sugar and syrup, then stir in the oats and ginger. Press into a greased 20 cm/8 in square cake tin (pan) and bake in a preheated oven at 180°C/350°F/gas mark 4 for about 20 minutes until lightly golden. Leave to cool slightly before cutting into bars, then leave in the tin to cool completely before turning out.

Nutty Flapjacks

Makes 16

75 g/3 oz/1/3 cup butter or margarine

50 g/2 oz/3 tbsp golden (light corn) syrup

100 g/4 oz/½ cup soft brown sugar

175 g/6 oz/1½ cups rolled oats

100 g/4 oz/1 cup chopped mixed nuts

Melt the butter or margarine with the syrup and sugar, then stir in the oats and nuts. Press into a greased 20 cm/8 in square cake tin (pan) and bake in a preheated oven at 180°C/350°F/gas mark 4 for about 20 minutes until lightly golden. Leave to cool slightly before cutting into bars, then leave in the tin to cool completely before turning out.

Sharp Lemon Shortbreads

Makes 16

100 g/4 oz/1 cup plain (all-purpose) flour

100 g/4 oz/½ cup butter or margarine, softened

75 g/3 oz/½ cup icing (confectioners') sugar, sifted

2.5 ml/½ tsp baking powder

A pinch of salt

30 ml/2 tbsp lemon juice

10 ml/2 tsp grated lemon rind

Blend together the flour, butter or margarine, icing sugar and baking powder. Press into a greased 23 cm/9 in square cake tin (pan) and bake in a preheated oven at 180°C/350°F/gas mark 4 for 20 minutes.

Mix together the remaining ingredients and beat until light and fluffy. Spoon over the hot base, reduce the oven temperature to 160°C/325°F/gas mark 3 and return to the oven for a further 25 minutes until springy to the touch. Leave to cool, then cut into squares.

Mocha and Coconut Squares

Makes 20

1 egg

100 g/4 oz/½ cup caster (superfine) sugar

100 g/4 oz/1 cup plain (all-purpose) flour

10 ml/2 tsp baking powder

A pinch of salt

75 ml/5 tbsp milk

75 g/3 oz/1/3 cup butter or margarine, melted

15 ml/1 tbsp cocoa (unsweetened chocolate) powder

2.5 ml/½ tsp vanilla essence (extract)

For the topping:

75 g/3 oz/½ cup icing (confectioners') sugar, sifted

50 g/2 oz/¼ cup butter or margarine, melted

45 ml/3 tbsp hot strong black coffee

15 ml/1 tbsp cocoa (unsweetened chocolate) powder

2.5 ml/½ tsp vanilla essence (extract)

25 g/1 oz/¼ cup desiccated (shredded) coconut

Beat together the eggs and sugar until light and fluffy. Stir in the flour, baking powder and salt alternately with the milk and melted butter or margarine. Stir in the cocoa and vanilla essence. Spoon the mixture into a greased 20 cm/8 in square cake tin (pan) and bake in a preheated oven at 200°C/400°F/gas mark 6 for 15 minutes until well risen and springy to the touch.

To make the topping, mix together the icing sugar, butter or margarine, coffee, cocoa and vanilla essence. Spread over the warm cake and sprinkle with coconut. Leave to cool in the tin, then turn out and cut into squares.

Hello Dolly Cookies

Makes 16

100 g/4 oz/½ cup butter or margarine

100 g/4 oz/1 cup digestive biscuit (Graham cracker) crumbs

100 g/4 oz/1 cup chocolate chips

100 g/4 oz/1 cup desiccated (shredded) coconut

100 g/4 oz/1 cup walnuts, chopped

400 g/14 oz/1 large can condensed milk

Melt the butter or margarine and stir in the biscuit crumbs. Press the mixture into the base of a greased and foil-lined 28 x 18 cm/11 x 7 in cake tin (pan). Sprinkle with the chocolate chips, then the coconut and, finally, the walnuts. Pour the condensed milk over the top and bake in a preheated oven at 180°C/350°F/ gas mark 4 for 25 minutes. Cut into bars while still warm, then leave to cool completely.

Nut and Chocolate Coconut Bars

Makes 12

75 g/3 oz/¾ cup milk chocolate

75 g/3 oz/¾ cup plain (semi-sweet) chocolate

75 g/3 oz/1/3 cup crunchy peanut butter

75 g/3 oz/¾ cup digestive biscuit (Graham cracker) crumbs

75 g/3 oz/¾ cup walnuts, crushed

75 g/3 oz/¾ cup desiccated (shredded) coconut

75 g/3 oz/¾ cup white chocolate

Melt the milk chocolate in a heatproof bowl set over a pan of gently simmering water. Spread over the base of a 23 cm/7 in square cake tin (pan) and leave to set.

Gently melt the plain chocolate and peanut butter over a low heat, then stir in the biscuit crumbs, walnuts and coconut. Spread over the set chocolate and chill until set.

Melt the white chocolate in a heatproof bowl set over a pan of gently simmering water. Drizzle over the biscuits in a pattern, then leave to set before cutting into bars.

Nutty Squares

Makes 12

75 g/3 oz/¾ cup plain (semi-sweet) chocolate

50 g/2 oz/¼ cup butter or margarine

100 g/4 oz/½ cup caster (superfine) sugar

2 eggs

5 ml/1 tsp vanilla essence (extract)

75 g/3 oz/¾ cup plain (all-purpose) flour

2.5 ml/½ tsp baking powder

100 g/4 oz/1 cup chopped mixed nuts

Melt the chocolate in a heatproof bowl over a pan of gently simmering water. Stir in the butter until melted, then stir in the sugar. Remove from the heat and beat in the eggs and vanilla essence. Fold in the flour, baking powder and nuts. Spoon the mixture into a greased 25 cm/10 in square cake tin (pan) and bake in a preheated oven at 180°C/350°F/ gas mark 4 for 15 minutes until golden. Cut into small squares while still warm.

Orange Pecan Slices

Makes 16

375 g/13 oz/3¼ cups plain (all-purpose) flour

275 g/10 oz/1¼ cups caster (superfine) sugar

5 ml/1 tsp baking powder

75 g/3 oz/1/3 cup butter or margarine

2 eggs, beaten

175 ml/6 fl oz/¾ cup milk

200 g/7 oz/1 small can mandarins, drained and coarsely chopped

100 g/4 oz/1 cup pecan nuts, chopped

Finely grated rind of 2 oranges

10 ml/2 tsp ground cinnamon

Mix together 325 g/12 oz/3 cups of the flour, 225 g/8 oz/1 cup of the sugar and the baking powder. Melt 50 g/2 oz/ ¼ cup of the butter or margarine and stir in the eggs and milk. Mix the liquid gently into the dry ingredients until smooth. Fold in the mandarins, pecan nuts and orange rind. Pour into a greased and lined 30 x 20 cm/12 x 8 in baking tin (pan). Rub together the remaining flour, sugar, butter and the cinnamon and sprinkle over the cake. Bake in a preheated oven at 180°C/350°F/gas mark 4 for 40 minutes until golden. Leave to cool in the tin, then cut into about 16 slices.

Parkin

Makes 16 squares

100 g/4 oz/½ cup lard (shortening)

100 g/4 oz/½ cup butter or margarine

75 g/3 oz/1/3 cup soft brown sugar

100 g/4 oz/1/3 cup golden (light corn) syrup

100 g/4 oz/1/3 cup black treacle (molasses)

10 ml/2 tsp bicarbonate of soda (baking soda)

150 ml/¼ pt/2/3 cup milk

225 g/8 oz/2 cups wholemeal (wholewheat) flour

225 g/8 oz/2 cups oatmeal

10 ml/2 tsp ground ginger

2.5 ml/½ tsp salt

Melt together the lard, butter or margarine, sugar, syrup and treacle in a pan. Dissolve the bicarbonate of soda in the milk and stir into the pan with the remaining ingredients. Spoon into a greased and lined 20 cm/8 in square cake tin (pan) and bake in a preheated oven at 160°C/325°F/gas mark 3 for 1 hour until firm. It may sink in the middle. Leave to cool, then store in an airtight container for a few days before cutting into squares and serving.

Peanut Butter Bars

Makes 16

100 g/4 oz/1 cup butter or margarine

175 g/6 oz/1¼ cups plain (all-purpose) flour

175 g/6 oz/¾ cup soft brown sugar

75 g/3 oz/1/3 cup peanut butter

A pinch of salt

1 small egg yolk, beaten

2.5 ml/½ tsp vanilla essence (extract)

100 g/4 oz/1 cup plain (semi-sweet) chocolate

50 g/2 oz/2 cups puffed rice cereal

Rub the butter or margarine into the flour until the mixture resembles breadcrumbs. Stir in the sugar, 30 ml/ 2 tbsp of the peanut butter and the salt. Stir in the egg yolk and vanilla essence and mix until well blended. Press into a 25 cm/10 in square cake tin (pan). Bake in a preheated oven at 160°C/325°F/gas mark 3 for 30 minutes until risen and springy to the touch.

Melt the chocolate in a heatproof bowl over a pan of gently simmering water. Remove from the heat and stir in the remaining peanut butter. Stir in the cereal and mix well until coated in the chocolate mixture. Spoon over the cake and level the surface. Leave to cool, then chill and cut into bars.

Picnic Slices

Makes 12

225 g/8 oz/2 cups plain (semi-sweet) chocolate

50 g/2 oz/¼ cup butter or margarine, softened

100 g/4 oz/½ cup caster sugar

1 egg, lightly beaten

100 g/4 oz/1 cup desiccated (shredded) coconut

50 g/2 oz/1/3 cup sultanas (golden raisins)

50 g/2 oz/¼ cup glacé (candied) cherries, chopped

Melt the chocolate in a heatproof bowl set over a pan of gently simmering water. Pour into the base of a greased and lined 30 x 20 cm/12 x 8 in Swiss roll tin (jelly roll pan). Cream together the butter or margarine and sugar until light and fluffy. Gradually add the egg, then mix in the coconut, sultanas and cherries. Spread over the chocolate and bake in a preheated oven at 150°C/300°F/gas mark 3 for 30 minutes until golden brown. Leave to cool, then cut into bars.

Pineapple and Coconut Bars

Makes 20

1 egg

100 g/4 oz/½ cup caster (superfine) sugar

75 g/3 oz/¾ cup plain (all-purpose) flour

5 ml/1 tsp baking powder

A pinch of salt

75 ml/5 tbsp water

For the topping:

200 g/7 oz/1 small can pineapple, drained and chopped

25 g/1 oz/2 tbsp butter or margarine

50 g/2 oz/¼ cup caster (superfine) sugar

1 egg yolk

25 g/1 oz/¼ cup desiccated (shredded) coconut

5 ml/1 tsp vanilla essence (extract)

Beat together the egg and sugar until light and pale. Fold in the flour, baking powder and salt alternately with the water. Spoon into a greased and floured 18 cm/7 in square cake tin (pan) and bake in a preheated oven at 200°C/ 400°F/gas mark 6 for 20 minutes until well risen and springy to the touch. Spoon the pineapple over the warm cake. Warm the remaining topping ingredients in a small pan over a low heat, stirring continuously until well blended without allowing the mixture to boil. Spoon over the pineapple, then return the cake to the oven for a further 5 minutes until the topping turns golden brown. Leave to cool in the tin for 10 minutes, then turn out on to a wire rack to finish cooling before cutting into bars.

Plum Yeast Cake

Makes 16

15 g/½ oz fresh yeast or 20 ml/4 tsp dried yeast

50 g/2 oz/¼ cup caster (superfine) sugar

150 ml/¼ pt/2/3 cup warm milk

50 g/2 oz/¼ cup butter or margarine, melted

1 egg

1 egg yolk

250 g/9 oz/2¼ cups plain (all-purpose) flour

5 ml/1 tsp finely grated lemon rind

675 g/1½ lb plums, quartered and stoned (pitted)

Icing (confectioners') sugar, sifted, for dusting

Ground cinnamon

Mix the yeast with 5 ml/1 tsp of the sugar and a little of the warm milk and leave in a warm place for 20 minutes until frothy. Whisk the remaining sugar and milk with the melted butter or margarine, the egg and egg yolk. Mix together the flour and lemon rind in a bowl and make a well in the centre. Gradually beat in the yeast mixture and the egg mixture to form a soft dough. Beat until the dough is very smooth and bubbles are beginning to form on the surface. Press gently into a greased and floured 25 cm/10 in square cake tin (pan). Arrange the plums close together over the top of the dough. Cover with oiled clingfilm (plastic wrap) and leave in a warm place for 1 hour until doubled in size. Place in a preheated oven at 200°C/400°F/gas mark 6, then immediately reduce the oven temperature to 190°C/375°F/gas mark 5 and bake for 45 minutes. Reduce the oven temperature again to 180°C/350°F/gas mark 4 and bake for a further 15 minutes until golden brown. Dust the cake with icing sugar and cinnamon while still hot, then leave to cool and cut into squares.

American Pumpkin Bars

Makes 20

2 eggs

175 g/6 oz/¾ cup caster (superfine) sugar

120 ml/4 fl oz/½ cup oil

225 g/8 oz cooked, diced pumpkin

100 g/4 oz/1 cup plain (all-purpose) flour

5 ml/1 tsp baking powder

5 ml/1 tsp ground cinnamon

2.5 ml/½ tsp bicarbonate of soda (baking soda)

50 g/2 oz/1/3 cup sultanas (golden raisins)

Cream Cheese Icing

Beat the eggs until light and fluffy, then beat in the sugar and oil and stir in the pumpkin. Beat in the flour, baking powder, cinnamon and bicarbonate of soda until well blended. Stir in the sultanas. Spoon the mixture into a greased and floured 30 x 20 cm/12 x 8 in Swiss roll tin (jelly roll pan) and bake in a preheated oven at 180°C/350°F/gas mark 4 for 30 minutes until a skewer inserted in the centre comes out clean. Leave to cool, then spread with cream cheese icing and cut into bars.

Quince and Almond Bars

Makes 16

450 g/1 lb quinces

50 g/2 oz/¼ cup lard (shortening)

50 g/2 oz/¼ cup butter or margarine

100 g/4 oz/1 cup plain (all-purpose) flour

30 ml/2 tbsp caster (superfine) sugar

About 30 ml/2 tbsp water

For the filling:

75 g/3 oz/1/3 cup butter or margarine, softened

100 g/4 oz/½ cup caster (superfine) sugar

2 eggs

A few drops of almond essence (extract)

100 g/4 oz/1 cup ground almonds

25 g/1 oz/¼ cup plain (all-purpose) flour

50 g/2 oz/½ cup flaked (slivered) almonds

Peel, core and slice the quinces thinly. Place in a pan and just cover with water. Bring to the boil and simmer for about 15 minutes until soft. Drain off any excess water.

Rub the lard and butter or margarine into the flour until the mixture resembles breadcrumbs. Stir in the sugar. Add just enough water to mix to a soft dough, then roll out on a lightly floured surface and use to line the base and sides of a 30 x 20 cm/12 x 8 in Swiss roll tin (jelly roll pan). Prick all over with a fork. Using a slotted spoon, arrange the quinces over the pastry.

Cream together the butter or margarine and sugar, then gradually beat in the eggs and almond essence. Fold in the ground almonds and flour and spoon over the quinces. Sprinkle the slivered almonds over the top and bake in a preheated oven at 180°C/350°F/gas mark 4 for 45 minutes until firm and golden brown. Cut into squares when cool.

Raisin Bars

Makes 12

175 g/6 oz/1 cup raisins

250 ml/8 fl oz/1 cup water

75 ml/5 tbsp oil

225 g/8 oz/1 cup caster (superfine) sugar

1 egg, lightly beaten

200 g/7 oz/1¾ cups plain (all-purpose) flour

1.5 ml/¼ tsp salt

5 ml/1 tsp bicarbonate of soda (baking soda)

5 ml/1 tsp ground cinnamon

2.5 ml/½ tsp grated nutmeg

2.5 ml/½ tsp ground allspice

A pinch of ground cloves

50 g/2 oz/½ cup chocolate chips

50 g/2 oz/½ cup walnuts, chopped

30 ml/2 tbsp icing (confectioners') sugar, sifted

Bring the raisins and water the boil, then add the oil, remove from the heat and leave to cool slightly. Stir in the caster sugar and egg. Mix together the flour, salt, bicarbonate of soda and spices. Blend with the raisin mixture, then stir in the chocolate chips and walnuts. Spoon into a greased 30 cm/12 in square cake tin (pan) and bake in a preheated oven at 190°C/ 375°F/gas mark 5 for 25 minutes until the cake begins to shrink away from the sides of the tin. Leave to cool before dusting with icing sugar and cutting into bars.

Raspberry Oat Squares

Makes 12

175 g/6 oz/¾ cup butter or margarine

225 g/8 oz/2 cups self-raising (self-rising) flour

5 ml/1 tsp salt

175 g/6 oz/1½ cups rolled oats

175 g/6 oz/¾ cup caster (superfine) sugar

300 g/11 oz/1 medium can raspberries, drained

Rub the butter or margarine into the flour and salt, then stir in the oats and sugar. Press half the mixture into a greased 25 cm/10 in square baking tin (pan). Scatter the raspberries over the top and cover with the remaining mixture, pressing down well. Bake in a preheated oven at 200°C/400°F/gas mark 6 for 20 minutes. Leave to cool slightly in the tin before cutting into squares.

www.ingramcontent.com/pod-product-compliance
Lightning Source LLC
Chambersburg PA
CBHW071817080526
44589CB00012B/820